ISBN

Hardcase 979-8-89556-365-6
Paperback 979-8-89556-265-9

BREAKING THE SILENCE

UNDERSTANDING DOMESTIC VIOLENCE AMONG MUSLIM WOMEN

DR. SABINA BEGAM AHMED & DR. ADITI NATH

notionpress.com

INDIA • SINGAPORE • MALAYSIA

Contents

Contents

List of Tables

Preface

This study investigates the experiences of Muslim women who are victims of domestic violence, focusing on the factors contributing to such violence, the impact of these factors on the victims, their perceptions of support services, and the challenges faced by these agencics in delivering assistance to the victims. This study was conducted in the Cachar district of Assam with 128 numbers of respondents selected through the census method from three organizations (DLCCIW, Sakhi One Stop Centre, Woodwichee-Swadhar Greh Home) that address domestic violence cases and provide support services. The methodology was qualitative and quantitative and, an interview schedule was used for data collection. The study had a two-way dimension that examined the issue of Domestic violence from both the viewpoints of the victims and the service providers.

The study findings revealed various factors that contribute to domestic violence, causing physical and emotional harm. Such violence has detrimental effects on family relations, sexual life, and children's well-being. In response, the respondents have approached service-providing agencies and, the agencies have extended all sorts of need-based services to the victims to resolve their problems. The majority of the respondents expressed their satisfaction with the services provided to them. Yet few suggestions were recommended by the victims to improve the service delivery of the select organizations. In addition, the service providers have also highlighted a few points that are challenging the smooth delivery of the services. The study has suggested a few measures for improving the condition of Muslim Women victims of domestic violence and service delivery of service-providing agencies.

The study advocates for more and morc initiatives to generate awareness about domestic violence and emphasizes the need to bring unregistered cases to the notice of the concerned organization so that registration of cases can be done to ensure support services. The study also emphasized capturing the experiences of male partners to gain a comprehensive understating of domestic violence dynamics in future research.

Chapter - 1

Introduction

The family is considered to be an abode of love, peace, and security for its members, which is commonly believed by the people across every culture and tradition. But this belief turns out to be a 'myth' for most of the families when the members of these families fall prey to the victimization of various crimes which mostly affect women and children. They are in danger of various types of viciousness at all ages, from pre-birth sex determination to maltreatment of widows and old ladies. The changing nature of women and girls association with family members, relatives, peers, authorities, and so on and the various conditions like at home, in school, at work, in society, and so forth in which they invest time and energy uncover women and child to explicit types of brutality during each period of their life. (Council of Europe, 2000). Since the Nineteen Nineties, there has been a growing worry about savagery against ladies overall and aggressive behavior at home specifically, in both created and non-industrial nations. Studies conducted in various regions of the planet showed the way up of cases of aggrieved behavior at home during pandemic. There has been an increment in calls to aggressive behavior at home assistance lines in numerous nations like China, France, Spain, Italy, and the United Kingdom (Taub, 2020) because of the flare-up of COVID 19 (UN Women 2020).

Violence in any form affects women irrespective of their socio-economic and cultural backgrounds. It affects women's wellbeing, hampers women's capacity to take an interest completely in the public eye. It has effects on sexual life and reproductive wellbeing of a woman. Altogether violence induces enormous physical and mental agony to a woman and their families as indicated by a review led by the US Department of Justice in 1991, men are answerable for 95% of attacks against companions or ex-life partners. In accordance to the committee on the elimination of discrimination against women domestic violence is a gender-based brutality which has unfair nature that disables the common liberties and key opportunities that a woman has like i) right to life, ii) not to be liable to torment or too awful, iii) not to encounter cruel or corrupting treatment or discipline, iv) freedom and security of individual v) to appreciate equivalent insurance under the law, vi) and to the best quality achievable of physical and emotional well-being (United Nations).

The National Family Health Survey III (NFHS) conducted in twenty nine states during 2005-06 observed a considerable number of wedded women had encountered physical and sexual maltreatment eventually of time in their lives by their spouses. The study mirrored that cross country 37.2% of ladies have encountered viciousness later marriage. During NFHS 2015-16, physical violence was reported by 21.5 percent of Muslim women in India. According to the survey, Jain women are the safest among religious communities, with only 9.3 percent of them experiencing physical assault.

Domestic violence across the communities is perceived as a human rights issue and is a serious problem in a majority of Muslim nations. Muslim feminists are of the opinion that the exact figure of such an issue is unknown to people since women hide the evidence of abuse and don't report it to authorities when they feel it is high. The adverse consequence of abuse that has on the sexual, reproductive health and rights of women were duly recognized by the national commission meant for women's development. Understanding the reality, the commission viewed that ensuring and satisfying conceptive privileges is an important condition for accomplishing sexual orientation and strengthening women to enable their ability in the entirety so that they can partake common liberties, essential opportunities and preclude cruelty against women.

1.1 Violence against Women

Violence against women or sex-based brutality is a complex worldwide issue recognized as the most genuine type of infringement of women's common freedom. The Declaration on the Elimination of Violence against Women in 1993 portrays "Brutality against ladies" as any exhibit of sex-based hostility that results in, or is most likely going to carry, physical, sexual or mental harm or suffering to women in broad day light or in personal life. The World Health Organization (1996) described violence as a deliberate use of real power against oneself, another person, or in a social occasion or in neighbourhood, either result in or have a high likelihood of causing injury, passing, mental harm, or difficulty.

The Council of Europe Convention on Violence against Women (Istanbul Convention 2011) emphasized brutality from gender point of view and expressed that issues related to sex equality should be well considered to address viciousness against women. The Istanbul Convention outlines the abolition of savagery against women with regards to accomplishing justice for women and underlines the structural nature of cruelty which is both a reason and an outcome of inconsistent power relations that restrict the progression of women. Besides, the development of sex-based roles and gender-based stereotypes in the general public shows that women have far lesser admittance to assets and direction when contrasted with men, resulting in an imbalanced equilibrium of influence. Inconsistent treatment and separation in kid raising; caring practices in the family, male inclination, and rejection of freedoms to medical care and schooling to women and young girls are a portion of the variables that make women defenceless and vulnerable to various types of brutality.

The worldwide data on viciousness against women reflected that in every three women, one globally encounters violence by an intimate partner in the course of life span (World Health Organisation, 2017). United Nations report shows that 18% of ladies and young ladies matured 15 to 49 years who at any point were engaged with a man, faced actual violence by the concerned person in the preceding year (UNDOCS, 2019). It is observed that 38% of women get murdered by their husbands (World Health Organisation, 2017). The statistics don't represent the wide range of various types of VAW for example inappropriate behavior, grabbing, and kidnapping.

Notwithstanding worldwide and public endeavors, like the Sustainable Development Goals (SGDs) and National Plan of Actions, which set out open doors for disposal of VAW, ventures stay deficient. Besides, the stoppage of the worldwide economy has additionally constrained states and givers to make significant decreases in financing issues related to violence against women. (Towers and Walby, 2015). The COVID 19 induced cross country restrictions expanded abusive behaviour at home uncovered the mistakes associated with gender orientation uniformity which needs earnest consideration and failure to resolve the matter now will cause massive expense in the future. (United Nations Women, 2020).

The National Family Health Survey (NFHS), India (2015-16), reflected that 29.5% of ladies encountered actual viciousness since age 15. The report of the National Crime Records Bureau (NCRB) highlighted that on average 87 cases of assaults were registered daily during 2019.(NCRB 2020).

1.1.1 Violence against Women in Assam

The state of Assam has become the hotbed for crime against women. Notwithstanding the means taken by the public authority to forestall violence, it keeps on being evil in society. Assam is one of the states of the North Eastern Region which paints a different picture in contrast with the rest of the North-East as far as a crime against women is concerned. Assam recorded the most elevated place of crime against women in the country for the fourth continuous year; uncover National Crime Records Bureau (NCRB) figures for 2020. The NCRB information shows that 11,408 instances of violence by spouses or family members were enlisted for 2020 in Assam. The increment in violations against ladies is additionally found in the National Family Health Survey-5 (NFHS) 2019-20. A similar picture clarifies that ladies in Assam experience more spousal violence than ladies at the public level (National Family Health Survey 3).

Table 1.1. Crime against women (2005-2020)

Heads of crime	Rape	Trafficking	Dowrydeath	Cruelty by husband	Kidnapping of women/girl	Molestation
2005	1238	25	99	2206	1456	899
2006	1244	29	105	2548	1544	1290
2007	1437	21	100	3000	1471	789
2008	1438	27	103	3478	1789	1272
2009	1631	37	170	4398	2092	1342
2010	1721	25	175	5410	2767	1400
2011	1700	21	121	5246	3192	1193
2012	1716	30	140	6407	3360	1840
2013	1937	18	170	8636	4222	2409
2014	2047	29	188	9626	3895	2641
2015	1852	47	216	11225	5039	3794
2016	1779	65	157	9321	5339	2701
2017	1708	79	150	10580	5186	3595
2018	1909	70	166	11999	6269	4143
2019	1952	49	165	13320	6326	4359
2020	1736	53	124	11389	4792	3820

Source: Government of Assam, Home & Political, Assam Police 2020

The comparison between public and state-level violence against women by the spouse shows 15.6% of women in Assam is a victim of emotional viciousness while this rate for all India remains at 15.8 and when 35.1 percent of ladies all over India faced physical violence then 36.7 percent women of Assam faced it. The level of sexual savagery against ladies in Assam is 14.8 whereas ladies in India face 10.0 percent. In addition, the range of physical or sexual violence in India is 37.2% and in Assam 39.5%. Assam experienced 42.1% emotional or physical or sexual violence in contrast to 39.7% at all Indian levels. Almost one-fourth (24%) of ladies matured 15-49 Assam have encountered physical or sexual brutality (National Family Health Survey 4).

In a review directed by North East Networks (NEN), an NGO, working for women's privileges had brought into notice the frightening condition of the state's provincial regions. It has been observed that 83.7% of ladies were truly manhandled by a relative, spouse, or business. The investigation additionally discovered that 34.1% of ladies had to sex. Other than going through actual maltreatment, ladies in provincial Assam have been viewed as experiencing verbal abuse by their spouses or parents in law for not bearing a youngster, particularly a male kid (NEN 2015).

Violence against women happens in various nature like i) violence at home; ii) assault and rape; iii) prostitution and dealing; iv) constrained marriage; v) female genital mutilation; vi) sexual aggravation.

These types of violence have consequences not only for the person who encounters it as well as their youngsters, families, and networks. Impacts of this violence can cause long haul physical and psychological well-being issues to the kids and families at micro level and can harm the communities by making community people job loss and homeless at meso level. Keeping in concern the gravity of the issue, thc present study will focus on domestic violence about Muslim women.

1.1.2 Domestic Violence

An exceptionally normal type of brutality that ladies are presented to is abusive behavior at home and is available in practically all social orders on the planet. There is no specific culture or strict gathering exempted from exploitation. It is portrayed as an abuse of the ability to control one more in a grown-up relationship including an example of conduct like physical, sexual, financial, and psychological mistreatment utilized alone or in a mix. Even many studies uncovered that women are essentially the sufferer of violence at home. (Green field 1998; Neubauer 1999, Rennison and Welchants 2000).

Domestic violence is described as an exhibition of maltreatment towards a wife by her companion or companions family members as stated by the Indian Penal Code, 498-A. Nonetheless, so far there was no such custom-based law-keeping an eye on the complexities of forceful conduct at home. Therefore, in 2006 an exhaustive legislation like protection of women from domestic violence Act 2005 became effective after having a long time of discussion and alterations. The prohibition of intimate attack and the issuance of safety and backing orders against partners and assistants who are internally and monetarily oppressive are key highlights of the regulation.

The Protection of Women from Domestic Violence Act, 2005, refers domestic violence to "any act, omission or commission or conduct of the respondent shall constitute domestic violence" in case it—

i) Harms or jeopardizes the security, life, appendage, prosperity, physical and mental wellbeing causing physical abuse, sexual abuse, verbal, emotional and economic abuse to the aggrieved person; or

ii) Pesters, hurts, harms, or imperils the abused individual to force her or some other individual connected with her to satisfy any unlawful need for any endowment or other property or significant security; or

iii) Has the effect of threatening the aggrieved person or any person related to her by any conduct mentioned in clause (a) or clause (b); or

iv) Damages or causes harm physically or mentally to the aggrieved person. (The Protection of Women from Domestic Violence Act 2005).

The Protection of Women from Domestic Violence Act, 2005 concedes specific privileges to women like-

i) The act gives a scope to the victim to live in a marital or shared family. She is entitled to get a house for her use and for that court can pass an order for getting her right of home in the family.

ii) A victim of domestic violence has the right of acquiring services and help from law enforcement agencies, security officers, shelter homes, medical and to record her grumbling under 498 A of the Indian Penal Code for wedding mercilessness.

iii) Under this Act a lady can get the accompanying requests given in support of herself through the courts once the offense of violence at home is set up-

    a) Orders on Protection- an order for preventing the abuser from committing or supporting abusive behaviour at home or workplaces of the aggrieved and setting up any sort of correspondence with her that may lead to disturbance can be passed by the court.

    b) Orders on Residence- The order guarantees that the possession of the aggrieved person has not been taken away, the common family isn't distanced or discarded. If required an alternative arrangement of accommodation could be made for the aggrieved where family members would be barred from entering the house allotted to her.

c) Orders on Custody- The order gives custody of children to the women victim or any individual approaching court for the custody of the child on her behalf or her. The order may allow victimizer to visit the children or may forbid assuming the visit might hurt the interest of the child or children.

d) Orders on Compensation- The abuser might be coordinated for the reimbursement of the damage or injuries caused to aggrieved women due to abusive behavior at home by the abuser. Such wounds further may add to mental torment and emotional stress to her.

1.1.3 Indicators of Domestic Violence

The Indicators of Domestic Violence are explained below:

i) Physical abuse: means any act or conduct which is of such a nature as to cause bodily pain, harm, or danger to life, limb, or health or impair the health or development of the aggrieved person and includes assault, criminal intimidation and criminal force;

ii) Sexual abuse: includes any conduct of a sexual nature that abuses, humiliates, degrades or otherwise violates the dignity of woman;

iii) Verbal and emotional abuse Includes— (a) insults, ridicule, humiliation, name calling and insults or ridicule specially with regard to not having a child or a male child; and (b) repeated threats to cause physical pain to any person in whom the aggrieved person is interested;

iv) Economic abuse includes— (a) deprivation of all or any economic or financial resources to which the aggrieved person is entitled under any law or custom whether payable under an order of a court or otherwise or which the aggrieved person requires out of necessity including, but not limited to, house hold necessities for the aggrieved person and her children, if any, stridhan, property, jointly or separately owned by the aggrieved person, payment of rental related to the shared house hold and maintenance; (b) disposal of household effects, any alienation of assets whether movable or immovable, valuables, shares, securities, bonds and the like or other property in which the aggrieved person has an interest or is entitled to use by virtue of the domestic relationship or which may be reasonably required by the aggrieved person or her children or her stridhan or any other property jointly or separately held by the aggrieved person; and (c) prohibition or restriction to continued access to resources or facilities which the aggrieved person is entitled to use or enjoy by virtue of the domestic relationship including access to the shared household (The Protection of Women from Domestic Violence Act 2005).

1.2 Pattern of Violence

The idea pattern of violence was created by a notable scientist Lenore Walker and she presented it in her book, The Battered Woman in 1979. As per her it is a tool to describe and understand the cyclical nature associated with battering and its effects on victims. It has three phases like i) tension stage; ii) Acute or Crisis stage; iii) Calm stage (Shelter 2021).

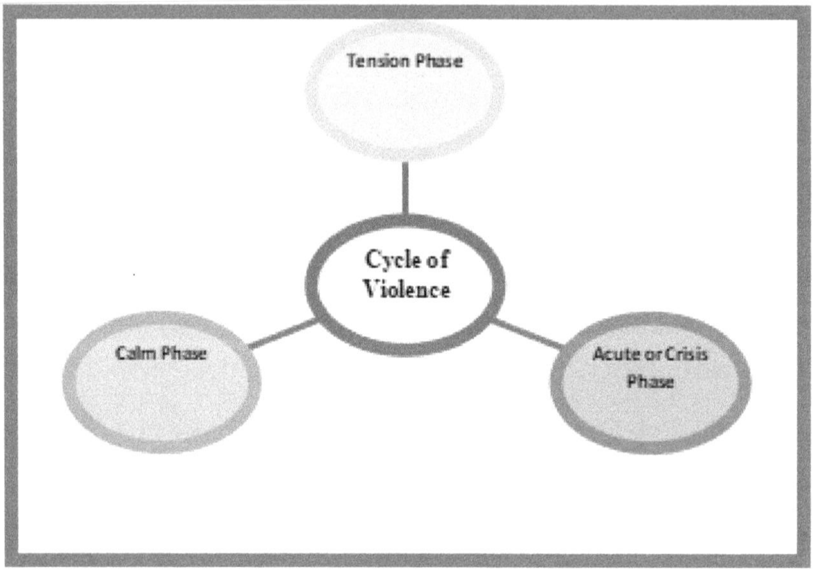

Diagram 1.1: Cycle of Violence

Phase 1: Tension stage

In this stage the victimizer tries to force his strength over the victim to control the victims' actions like victims are not allowed to contact family members; spend money to fulfill their requirement and they are made bound to take permission for everything they do which sometimes become difficult for victims to obey. In case of noncompliance, the abuser threatens the victim with dire consequences and thus the victim becomes subjected to physical, sexual, or psychological mistreatment because of the consequences. Such an act makes the marital relationship tenser. As a result, little acts of violence such as punching, slapping, or shoving become more frequent. Though the restrictions put forth are extremely hard to follow yet the victims try to act accordingly to avoid the inevitable assaults. The pair enters the following phase, the acute or crisis phase, after breaking the norms.

Phase II: Acute or Crisis Stage

The compromising nature of the victim put them in a more vulnerable situation. The dominant behavior of the abuser leads to more physical and intense emotional violence in this phase and a feeling of powerlessness develops in the victim to stop such violent behavior of the abuser. Some people who are enduring violence may initiate the beating event to "get it over with" and restore control. At this point, giving medical care and securing secure housing for the abused person is the best course of action.

Phase III: Calm Stage

The last phase of the abusive behavior at home cycle is the quiet stage. The stage is portrayed as objective coordinated, consistent and agreeable. It is expected that the victim will be responsive towards the decisions made by the abuser. The abuser makes an effort to gain forgiveness and continue with the relationship and therefore the abuser behaves very gently with the victim and makes promises for not doing such inhuman act in future. But the abuser tries to make the victim understand that the violence has taken place for the victim only. Victim is frequently provided with valuable gift items by the abuser to ensure forgiveness. The victim genuinely needs to accept that the maltreatment will reach a conclusion with the help, love and care of victimizer.

Victims of domestic violence have to gone through different phases of violence which initially creates a tensionised situation and later put them in crisis condition. But those come up from the chaotic situation using problem solving strategies, starts a new life. In some cases even after deliberate effort of making a healthy relationship, things does not turn up positively that affects women from all aspects.

For a woman disclosing the abusive experience and seeking treatment from the concerned support providing agency is not an easy task. Muslim women like different women might confront obstacles of various natures with regards to disclosing abusive relationship and getting aid. It was North American Council for Muslim Women, the first Muslim national organisation holding a national convention in 1993 on abuse &violence against Muslim women and Children. Subsequently, the Islamic Society of North America have organised conferences for led social specialist organizations in Plainfield, Indiana, in 1995 and Chicago the next year, covering a range of subjects like family therapy, divorce, and children's concerns.

1.3 Muslim Women and Domestic Violence

It has been observed in the literature that Muslim women in India are the most affected. Poverty is not the only source of Muslim women's struggle, which separates them from women of other communities. It includes communal conservatism, patriarchy, religious leaders, and the community's fear of losing their Islamic identity if they allow their children to pursue secular education, with a particular emphasis on preventing their girls from being exposed to modernity. Purdah is a distinctive aspect of Muslim women, and Muslim women's education is typically limited to religious knowledge. Illiteracy among them, as well as a lack of exposure to reality, had a negative impact on the community's socio-educational standing, pushing them deeper into poverty. Many middle-class women with the necessary qualifications are barred from seeking work because their 'community reputation' will be tarnished. As a result, Muslims in India, particularly Muslim women, are considered backward (Priscilla Offenhauer 2005).

The report of the Sachar Committee underlines the significance of community identity for Muslim ladies' standing. Women, by and large, are the torchbearers of the community when it is seen to be under danger or threat. It normally impacts ladies in sensational ways; ladies take on clear markers of local area ID with the rest of their personal effects and in their conduct, now and again of their longing, once in a while because of local area pressure. The women are unwilling to be a part of modernization initiative that threatens to blur community lines. It is said, "The only safe location (both in terms of physical safety and in terms of identity protection) for countless Muslim ladies in India now a days is inside the constraints of family and community."

Internal and external oppression is experienced by Muslim women. Muslim men oppress their wives and embrace any concept of change because they think it to be Islamic. Muslims are essentially craftsmen and independently employed, and they have a sociologically restricted perspective and live in their universe. Then, at that point, there are Muslims who live in rustic regions and work as agrarian workers and other related positions, which increases traditionalism as well as make the way for brutality against Muslim ladies. The continuance of patriarchal societal standards, and gender hierarchy, underpins the system. It is the women who have been oppressed and discriminated against not because of their gender only but also for issues like caste, class, ability, sexual orientation, tradition, and other factors. As a result, many people are exposed to a continuous cycle of violence throughout their lives, sometimes referred to as "from the birth to the grave."

Table 1.2: Violence against Women by any husband in Assam

Religion	Emotional Violence	Physical Violence	Sexual Violence	Physical or Sexual violence	Emotional, Physical & Sexual	Physical or sexual	Physical or sexual or emotional
Hindu	11.6	23.2	5.2	4.0	2.6	24.3	27.0
Muslim	11.4	20.1	5.4	4.2	2.7	21.3	24.4
Christian	11.6	22.2	5.2	3.9	2.4	23.4	26.7
Sikh	6.1	16.8	4.3	3.9	2.0	17.2	18.6
Buddhist	7.8	17.2	3.6	3.3	2.5	17.4	18.2
Jain	3.7	10.7	5.3	4.2	0.7	11.8	13.2
Other	7.7	22.7	7.2	6.1	4.4	23.8	24.7

Source: National Family Health Survey 2015-16

Viciousness against women is an after-effect of the social and institutional betrayal that most Indian women face. Despite the Government of India's various protective measures, Muslim women in India have not been freed from age-old traditions and practices, and hence are unable to contribute significantly to general progress. Emancipation could be a critical stage in the formation of a community. An improvement in their current situation will contribute not only to the community's growth and modernization but also to the nation's development and modernization.

1.4 Islam's View on Violence against Women

As indicated by 'Quaran', the essential message of Islam and the prophetic practice 'Sunnah' and 'Hadith', violence against women in Islam has never been upheld. The Quaran sees marriage for peacefulness and is a dividing liability among two parts of society which gives security, consolation, harmony, generosity, solace, equity, benevolence, love and increases emotional wellbeing and spiritual harmony. Hence, there is no scope for violence against women in Islam.Quaran has a whole part (4) on 'Ladies' depicting anticipated practices; code of morals; set of accepted rules; compromise concerning care, legacy, marriage, separation, struggle, etc.

Table 1.3: Violence against Women by their husbands in Assam

Religion	Emotional Violence	Physical Violence	Sexual Violence	Physical or Sexual Violence	Emotional, Physical or Sexual Violence
Hindu	14.0	30.5	6.7	31.7	34.0
Muslim	14.1	27.1	6.4	28.3	31.4
Christian	14.0	28.8	6.0	30.1	33.1
Sikh	6.8	19.2	5.0	19.5	20.9
Buddhist	9.7	22.7	4.1	22.8	23.4
Jain	4.8	10.7	5.3	11.8	14.3
Other	9.5	32.3	16.0	33.3	34.1

Source: National Family Health Survey 2015-16

As indicated by Muhammad, 'the best are those who are ideal to their spouses'Tirmidhi (Sahih). Prophet has portrayed husband's liability towards wives saying "you give her food when you take; you material her when you fabric yourself; you don't berate her face and don't beat her; she is your mate and mom of your youngsters." Based on such messages, Muslim researchers of the past and the current view all types of aggressive behavior at home as types of abuse and the Quaran and the hadith is unequivocal in his preclusion against all structures mistreatment, and is clearly expressed in sacred Quaran (Abdalla 2004). Still, some men misbehave with women knowing that they are disobeying Allah's guidance (Islamic Society of North America 2009). The Qur'an calls any individual who goes past Allah's limits as "offender."

1.4.1 Marriage & Divorce in Islam

1.4.1.1 Marriage:

Marriage in Islam is an agreement between a man and a woman who lives as a couple. From a religious point of view marriage is a devotional act-ibadat. Quran permits polygamy marriage however it is confined to a limit of four spouses. A Muslim man can have four spouses with a condition that all wives will be treated by the husband similarly as far as adoration, care, and regard is concerned. Uniformity is relied upon with respect to accounts, feelings and sexual connections. Assuming the spouse can't satisfy these conditions then he ought to wed once (Sahayak 2021). If the man marries the fifth one despite of having four wives, the marriage will turn out to be irregular. The fifth marriage will be valid only after the demise and termination of marriage of one of the four wives.

Some Muslim researchers think about that assuming an individual can wed and treat his better half appropriately and fears emphatically that he will participate in unlawful demonstrations assuming he doesn't, then, at that point, marriage for his situation is obligatory; another school of thought believes that if an individual doesn't have a sound monetary and actual means to wed or having a sort of feeling for not treating his wife properly then the marriage will be considered as forbidden. In situations where the individual possess the ability to marry yet has an overwhelming inclination that he won't treat his partner appropriately then the marriage will be known as a detested marriage. On the other hand, if an individual can wed and has no anxiety toward abusing his significant other or of committing unlawful demonstration assuming he doesn't wed, then, at that point, marriage for his situation is preferred.

Four unique conditions should be met at the hour of marriage in understanding to *Quaran:* i) conditions needed for starting the agreement, ii) conditions needed for the sufficiency of the agreement, iii) conditions needed for carrying out the agreement, & iv) conditions needed to make the wedding restricting.

To begin the marriage cycle, the prospective couple should have to meet the legal competence for the purpose and lady can't be from those classifications that are taboo for man to wed. To have a sound agreement few conditions are to be met. Some of which are concurred and acknowledged by the researchers however others are for certain conflicts. The conditions are: i) the lady is admissible to the man; ii) the proposition and acknowledgment is of a long-lasting nature and not impermanent; iii) somewhere around two non-defamed observers; iv) the two parties involved in the agreement and the lady specifically have enthusiastically acknowledged the marriage; v) the lady and husband are to be explicitly recognized and known; vi) neither of the marriage parties should be in a condition of ihraam; vii) the marriage ought to be with a settlement (mahr); viii) the social events and observers will without a doubt keep it quiet; ix) attendance of the women's delegate.

To precede with the agreement both the couple should be lawfully competent for example the two of them ought to be normal, cognizant, accomplished and so on. The agreement can occur before marriage yet execution should delay until the couple go into a conjugal relationship. Once the conditions are met, neither parties will have the option to revoke the agreement that mentions husband is social and eligible for the women and there is no deformation in either mate. If these conditions are not met, the matter can be brought to the notice of legal personnel's. When the marriage is acknowledged by both the parties with needs it contains in the relationship, they will undoubtedly keep up with such marriage.

In Muslim society a couple have more prominent privileges and commitments towards one another because of the agreement executed between them for carrying on with coexistence. The two mates have the accompanying privileges over the other:

The right to appreciate with each other (Baqarah, 2:223; Nisaa, 4:20-21)

i) The right to gain from each other (Nisaa, 4:11-12)
ii) The right of affirming the heredity of their kids (Bukhari and Muslim)

The privileges that a Muslim wife has over the spouse are as per the following:

i) Settlement (mahr) (Nisaa, 4:4)
ii) Support/upkeep (Baqarah, 2:223; Nisaa, 4:34)
iii) Kind and proper treatment (40 Nisaa, 4:19)
iv) Marital relations (Bukhari and Muslim)
v) Not to be beaten (Nisaa, 4:34; Bukhari)
vi) Privacy (Abu Dawud)
vii) Justice between various spouses (Nisaa, 4:129; Abu Dawud)
viii) To be shown her religion (Tahreem, 66:6; Bukhari)

The privileges that a husband has over the spouse are as per the following:

i) Have a home with a favorable family climate in which both can live respectivelywithout a hitch, cheerfully and pleasantly. (A"araaf, 7:189; Rum, 30:21)
ii) To be treated as head of the family (Nisaa, 4:34)
iii) To be answerable to conjugal relations (Tirmidhi)
iv) Not to permit anybody in the house whom he objects (Bukhari and Muslim)
v) Not to take off from the house without his approval (Ahzaab, 33:33)
vi) That she cooks for him, keep his home and appropriately manage the family(Ahmad; Bukhari and Muslim)
vii) That she stays dependable, reliable and dedicated (Nasaa"i)
viii) Express gratitude for his endeavors and not to be gone up with too many interest (Bukhari and Muslim; Nasaa"i; Haakim).

1.4.1.2 Classification of Muslim Marriage

Muslim marriage has been classified in the following classes:(SyedaShajiaSharmin,Dr. Mir Mohammad Azad: 2018)

i) Sahih (valid) Marriage
ii) Batil (void) Marriage
iii) Fasid (Irregular) Marriage
iv) Muta Marriage

1.4.1.2.1 Sahih (valid) Marriage:

A valid marriage is the most legitimate kind of marriage performed following all legal requirements and which is free from prohibitions affecting the parties. The children born from this union are legal. The husband is obligated to pay Mahar as a dower to his wife. The spouse is allowed to get support from her partner.

1.4.1.2.2 Batil (void) Marriage:

A batil wed is an illicit weeding according to Islam which does not create any right or obligation between the parties. Such marriage does not have dower, iddah and legitimacy. The children born from such a union are illegitimate.

1.4.1.2.3 Fasid (irregular) Marriage:

The two parties when don't meet the vital necessities for a real marriage are called irregular marriage. The following marriages are considered irregular: a) Absence of required number of an observer during marriage contract; b) marriage with women during her Iddat period; c) A marriage with women without the assent of her custodian when such assent is viewed as fundamental; d) A marriage restricted because of distinction of religion; e) A marriage with women who is pregnant when the pregnancy was not brought about by infidelity or sex; f) A marriage with a fifth spouse.

1.4.1.2.4 Muta Marriage:

The Muta marriage is done for a fixed period. It is lawful in the Shia sect. The marriage gets disintegrated in itself on the lapse of the term of the marriage. It is assumed that if the time limit isn't communicated, the marriage is affirmed to be long-lasting. Regarding dower should be mentioned in the agreement of Muta marriage in any case otherwise the understanding is void.

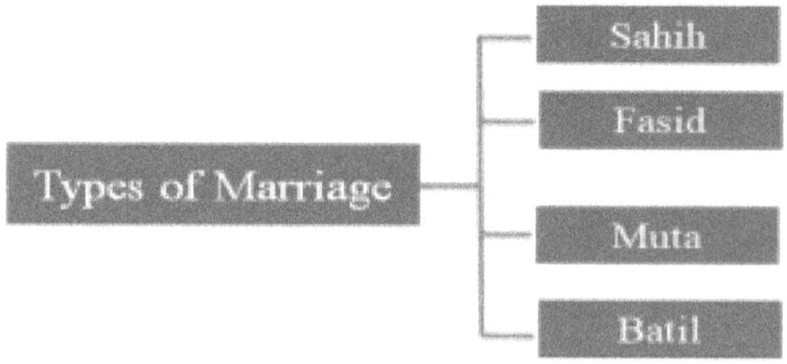

Diagram 1.2: Types of Muslim Marriage

1.4.2 Divorce in Islam

Islam does not encourage divorce but most Muslim scholar view divorce as a better option for those who are not happy in their matrimonial relationship and their relationship has broken down because of any reason. Islam prefers the reunion of two conflicting parties and to cancel divorce during the reconciliation time. It allows divorce only when it is understood that living together in harmony for both the couples would be impossible and all sorts of efforts made to bring peace in the relationship but could not yield any positive result. The divorce procedure/arbitration procedure/before the actual termination of marriage/follows different steps likes:

i) Both the couples should attempt to settle their disparities all alone (Nisaa, 4:19; Baqarah, 2:228)

ii) If they fall flat, two mediators, one each from a couple's side will be designated to put forth fundamental attempts for settling the distinctions (Nisaa, 4:35)

iii) If this endeavor falls flat, then the spouse or the wife might look for a separation (Baqarah, 2:236, 229, 237; 231)

iv) And if separation occurs, a compromise and re-examination season of 90 days is accessible (aside from assuming the gatherings have separated from one another for the third time) (Talaq, 65:1; Baqarah, 2:228)

v) If no compromise happens with in the mentioned time frame then the separation turns out to be viable and marriage gets ended (Baqarah, 2:229).

It is the case that in Islam "power" of separation lies in the possession of the spouse, not in the wife. In any case, this doesn't imply that the spouse is confined to stop the marriage when she is abused, unsatisfied and miserable. In such cases assuming separation is started by the women, it is called khula. There should be a holding up period to guarantee the woman isn't pregnant.

Introduction

The idea of separation fluctuates as indicated by the circumstances. It tends to be i) reasonable (permissible), ii) terrible (detestable), iii) attractive (desirable), iv) required (obligatory), or v) denied (prohibited). Along these lines, it can include any of the super five decisions.

Divorce is admissible for spouse when he encounters the evil direct of wife, hurt brought about by wife to him and the non-satisfaction of the lawful target of marriage by his significant other in marriage. In cases where there is no such problem between the married couples, divorce is better to be denied, according to the Muslim scholars. In circumstances when spouse endure hurt in conjugal relationship and there is confllct between the couple which makes arrangement for the wife to hate husband then the separation becomes desirable for the husband.

If the spouse is found neither virtuous nor uprights on religious matters like she is neglectful towards performing prayers timely and husband is not able to correct her, in that situation becomes obligatory (Dogarawa, A. B. (2009). In Islam it is denied for the spouse to separate from his better half during her period wherein he has as of now had sex with her. Furthermore, the spouse is barred to separate from his better half threefold at once; (Talaaq, 65:1; Nisaa, 4:130). A separated woman or widow can marry again in Islam but they must have to observe a period of iddah (3 months) before remarrying to see whether they are pregnant from a previous marriage or not. If she is found pregnant then she must wait till delivery of the child before remarriage. A Muslim man has the permission for second marriage without divorcing the first wife. The same is not applicable for Muslim women. In order to marry another man, a Muslim woman has to go through a divorce proceeding under Muslim personal law or Muslim marriage act, 1939. If a Muslim lady marries for the second time while the first marriage subsists then that marriage will be considered invalid (Sahayak 2021)

In Islam, if the marriage goes wrong, both couples have equal rights to end the marriage by seeking and obtaining divorce. However, the picture does not appear to be that in practice. The social norms don't support the move of divorce by women. Any such move creates a flutter in the community. Often such women are branded as bad women and are exposed to severe mental, emotional and physical torture.

They even don't get support from their parents. During marriage a Muslim women (wife) is entitled to get Mehr. However, the divorced wife rarely gets the Mehr from her husband. Moreover, the amount of Mehr is not sufficient to maintain the life of wife after divorce. She is entitled for maintenance from her significant other just for the time of Iddat.

1.5 Theoretical Perspectives and correlates to domestic violence

Theories are useful tools for approaching a research problem. They not only present a certain point of view, but they also allow the researcher to conduct a methodical analysis of the study question. In the following paragraphs, discussion has been made on few relevant theories to understand the research problem from theoretical perspective and to correlate it with the practical context of present research.

Women's activist Theory (Feminist Theory)

Feminist theory centers on sexual orientation disparity and perceive that lady's experiences of social circumstances are diverse as well as inconsistent with men's. Feminist theory underscores sex and power, asserting that violence represents uneven power among people in the public arena. In almost all social institutions, including the family, the patriarchal structure of society plays a major role concerning domestic violence. (Afkhami, M., Ertürk, Y., & Mayer, A. E. 2019).

Psycho-Pathological Theory

The theory rotates around the character qualities of guilty parties and casualties. The hypothesis contains that the savagery is associated with psychological maladjustment, liquor, and other intra-individual peculiarities. This theory offers two separate clarifications: i) the reasons for savagery against ladies are brought about by the guilty party's mental troubles; and ii) the reasons for brutality against ladies are caused by the wrongdoer's mental issues (like burdensome imprudence, uncontrolled feelings, and so on). (S. Saeed., W.A. Muhammad., & K. Muhammad 2014).

Socio-Psychological Theories

As indicated by the socio-mental hypothesis, the most effective way to comprehend violence is to take a note of the outer natural factors that affect a wrongdoer. This hypothesis checks out the sorts of regular associations that lead to brutality (for instance, distressing circumstances or familial interactional examples). Assumptions like the frustration-aggression, perversion, and self-attitude check out viciousness against women from a socio-mental point of view, as nitty-gritty underneath (Sarah Mclachlan; Derwin King Chung Chan; David Keatley; Martin Hagger, 2011).

Frustration- Aggression Theory

John Dollard proposed this hypothesis in 1939. It explains how mental disturbance causes violence at home. It clarifies individual ill-feeling because the individual is the subject of serious individual commitment and familial dissatisfaction. When something does not get in the way of a person's attempt to achieve a goal or an end, he or she becomes frustrated, and frustration leads to aggression. This hypothesis was changed after considering numerous criticisms. Even if the temptation for violence is high after an unpleasant event, it is perceived that a real articulation of aggression can be stifled by either disguised guidelines or outer limitations. It is also acknowledged that irritation can build up over time and be active for a long time. The aggressive behavior is not always a result of frustration rather dependent on a variety of conditions (Sturmey, P. (Ed.). (2017).

Perversion Theory

Psychoanalysts utilize the 'Hypothesis of Perversion' and the 'Hypothesis of Symptom Formation' to clarify savagery. They don't believe degenerates are substandard individuals rather accept that depravity is the consequences of senses. Infantile features in perverts do not go through the typical integration process during puberty. According to this idea, violence might be the result of strong inborn urges or unhealthy events in childhood or adolescence (Binswanger, R. 2017).

Socio- Cultural Theories

These hypotheses reflect on the large-scale level evaluations of abusive behavior at home executed against relatives. Aggressive behavior at home is depicted as socially organized imbalances, socio-social perspective, and standards towards against social conduct, are connected in these thoughts. Underlying functional, resource, patriarchal, social learning, and exchange theory are a portion of the sub speculations that are explained further down (Zubaidi, N. 2015).

Structural–Functional Theory

The thought indicates that social groupings vary as far as common degrees of stress, hardship, and dissatisfaction are concerned. It contends that the people who are under a great deal of pressure and have a ton of assets are bound to be brutal. This thought portrays one's action at the backdrop of how they are framed and controlled by the societal structure.

Resource Theory

According to the Resource Theory of Violence, all social systems (including the family) rely on force or the fear of force to some extent. The more resources a person has—social, personal, and financial—the more power he or she can wield. According to William Goode (1971), the more resources a person has, the less likely he or she is to use force openly. So, if a spouse wants to be the dominant person in the household but has minimal education, a low-status and low-paying profession, lacks interpersonal skills, he may resort to violence to keep his position (Kazemi. A.,&Tornblom. K.Y., 2017).

Patriarchal Theory

The patriarchal theory made by Dobash and Dobashin in 1979, battles that male-controlled society prompts ladies' subjection and adds to a long history of methodical violence. The brutalization of a single woman (especially in the home) by a single man is an expression of historically and cross-culturally existing male dominance over women, not an individual and family problem. The social acceptance of 'wife abuse' reflects patriarchal standards that favor male authority in marriage. Men were prone to making a living for the family and held centers of authority, resources, property, and so on, whereas women were preoccupied with birthing and nursing children and therefore were reliant on men. As a result, there was an unequal allocation of power in the household. According to Dobash&Dobash, violence, male dominance, and female subjugation are valued in society (Akgul, F. 2017).

Social Learning Theory

As per the social learning hypothesis, individuals figure out the proper behavior by encountering and being presented with violence. As per this idea, kids who see viciousness between their parents or who have been mishandled as kids are more inclined to utilize brutality as grown-ups (Lyons, S. D., and Berge, Z. L. 2012).

Exchange theory

The essential reason of the 'Trade Theory' of viciousness is that human contact is roused by the craving for benefits while keeping away from discipline and expenses. People will involve power and force in their associations with intimates and relatives assuming that they accept the advantages of such conduct offset the disservices of such conduct (Cook, K. S., 2013).

Theories have given a wide scope to comprehend violence and domestic violence from an alternate perspective. Feminist theorists believe that gender inequality, gender oppression, put a section of women in a deceived condition. The personality characteristic, psychological problems of offenders, stressful situations, structural inequality, socio-cultural attitudes often lead to violence in the family environment. It has been perceived that numerous when things don't happen according to the wish of an individual, it prompts dissatisfaction and gets appeared through viciousness.As per the asset hypothesis, an individual having more assets is less inclined to utilize power to control the accomplice openly. The Indian social structure already has predefined gender-specific roles and responsibilities and the male-centric hypothesis has introduced the capacity of both sex by featuring men as providers and hence become the focal point of power, assets, property, etc. while ladies are engrossed with birthing and nursing kids and along these lines are dependent on men. The social learning hypothesis featured that individual's gain from encounters. If a youngster in his/her childhood encounters parental clash or violence, possibilities are there for the same child to employ violence in adulthood.It is perceived from the theories that no single theory can sufficiently explain the reasons for violence against women. In any case, it is seen that the most effective way to comprehend viciousness is to check out the natural elements of the guilty parties. The numerous dimension of violence helped the researcher to understand the problem all the more profoundly and relate it with the current study.

1.6 Provisions for Women: Constitutional & Legal

1.6.1 Constitutional provisions

The constitution of India has enshrined gender equality through basic freedoms & basic obligations. The constitution has granted rights to women and empowers the State to take on measures for uplifting women's condition in all aspects. Accordingly, development policies, plans, laws, schemes, and programs are introduced focussing on women's movement in different spheres. India has approved distinctive international instruments committed to getting equivalent privileges of women. Among others Elimination of All Forms of Discrimination against Women (CEDAW) 1936 is one.

Significant Constitutional arrangements connecting with women are referenced underneath

i) Uniformity in the eyes of law for women (Article 14)

ii) No discrimination with any resident on grounds of religion, race, station, sex, birth place Article 15 (I)

iii) Unique arrangements and plans can be made by the State for the protection of women and children Article 15 (3).

iv) All citizens are to be provided with equal employment opportunity to any states offices (Article 16)

v) All citizens irrespective of gender reserve the right to an adequate means of living 39 (A) and 39 (d) ensures equivalent remuneration for equivalent work for all kinds of people.

vi) The State is to make course of action for getting prompt and altruistic states of work and for parenthood help (Article 42).

vii) The academic and financial interests of the fragile segments of individuals shall be promoted by the State and shield them from social betrayal and mistreatment (Article 46).

viii) The degree of nourishment and way of life with better public health facilities shall be lifted up by the State (Article 47).

ix) Participation of ladies in Panchayati Raj Institutions commanding essentially 33% reservation for ladies out of an absolute number of seats that to be filled by direct political race (Article 243 D(3)

1.6.2 Legal Provisions

Remembering the Constitutional Provision for women, various women explicit laws have been sat back to time. A portion of the significant laws connecting with women are talked about under the accompanying heads:

The Child Marriage Restraint Act, 1929

By setting up an eligible age for the two genders, this Act forbids both girls and boys from marrying as children. It determines that the bride should be 18 years of age and the groom of the hour should be 21 years of age before they wed. Any grown-up male gets a child marriage, an individual who executes, leads, or coordinates the child marriage, and the guardian who empowers allows or solemnizes a child marriage are dependent upon punishments.

The Factories Act, 1948

The focal goal of the Act is to control working situations as far as wellbeing, security, and government assistance is concerned. It prohibits women from dealing with or close to moving machinery. No female specialist can be compelled to lift an extreme load by her boss, and she can't work the night shift. The Act mentioned separate urinals, lavatories for women. It further expresses that in workplaces having more than thirty women employees, the employer should facilitate women employees with a crèche so that adequate care can be provided to female employees' children who are under six years.

The Special Marriage Act, 1954

The Act monitors inter-caste and inter-religion marriages. The Act is endorsed based on the following conditions:

- Neither of the parties has a living spouse.
- Neither of the parties is affected with any mental disorder which proves unsuitable for marriage and the reproduction of kids

- Neitherparty is impacted with any psychological problem which renders them unsuitable
- The bride and the groom have achieved the age of 18 and 21 individually.

The Hindu Marriage Act, 1955

Hindu women's right to divorce is guided under this Act. The Act supports women to divorce their husbands by establishing a variety of grounds. For example, if a female is intellectually mishandled or abused by her spouse or has verbose episodes of mental sickness, this gives an obvious reason for separation under this Act.

The Immoral Traffic (Prevention) Act, 1956

The Act specifies the penalty for running whorehouse, dealing with people for prostitution, and living off a whore's benefits, in addition to other things. The Act prohibits prostitution in public places to protect public morals and society. Furthermore, it imposes severe penalties for crimes committed alongside by a youngster or an adolescent. Concerned authority like police has the ability to go into the matter and rescue people if the court so orders. Even the police is entrusted with the power of arresting the miscreants without a warrant. Each offense punished by the Act is a cognizable offense.

The Hindu Succession Act, 1956

The Act acknowledges women's privileges to acquire property on an equivalent balance with males. It underlines that a daughter has complete ownership of her parent's property like a son. All family members have equal rights in a Hindu male's self-acquired property, for example, his daughter(s), spouse, mother, girl's little girl, and bereaved little girl in-law.

The dowry prohibition Act, 1961

This law makes it unlawful to demand or accept dowry. Dowry is defined as a gift of goods, property, or else cash made by one or the other party to the marriage, or by the guardians or any other individual engaged with the marriage. Within India, this Act applies to people of all faiths. Inability to full-fill dowry demands used to invite specific types of violence to women. Thus the dowry prohibition act has mentioned the least and the extreme punishments that will be given to the concerned for giving and getting endowments.

The Maternity Benefit Act, 1961

The motivation behind the Act is to further develop the prosperity of working ladies.The Maternity Benefit Act of 1961 administers ladies' work at determining occasions like before and after delivery. It additionally accommodates maternity leave and the instalment of specific financial advantages to female representatives who can't work because of their pregnancy. It applies to any factory, mine, or plantation, including any government-owned or operated facility, as well as any establishment where people are engaged to perform equestrian, acrobatic, or other acts. According to the Act, ladies are precluded to work at any organization for quite some time following the day of their conveyance or unnatural birth cycle. The 2017 amendment raised maternity benefits, such as paid maternity leave, two months leave before the projected delivery date, 18 weeks leave after delivery. The 2017 amendment raised maternity benefits, such as paid maternity leave, 8 weeks leave before the delivery and 18 weeks after delivery. An employer might permit her to work from home later after the completion of the maternity benefit period.

The Medical Termination of Pregnancy Act, 1971

Pregnant women's psychological and physical wellbeing is guaranteed through this Act. It specifies the time, location, and circumstances under which a registered medical practitioner may terminate a pregnancy. This Act makes abortion legal in conditions where contraceptives fall flat and the pregnancy adversely affects the planned mother's physical or emotional wellness. In the event of terminating the pregnancy clinically, the consent of the pregnant woman is required.

The Equal Remuneration Act 1976

It stipulates that labourers of both genders get equal wages for the equivalent work without discrimination. Section 4 of the Act states that no business will pay any labourer remuneration that is less positive than that paid to labourers of the other gender, regardless of whether in real money or kind. The rate of remuneration of any worker shall not be reduced by the employer for performing the same or similar work.

The Commission of Sati (Prevention) Act, 1987

The Act expects to keep Sati from being submitted and celebrated. It specifies punishments for any person who, clearly or indirectly attempt to submit Sati or help in the exhibit of Sati. The Act disallows the worship of Sati and makes it illicit. The partner is barred from acquiring the property of the individual against whom the Sati is executed under this Act. Furthermore, the Act mandates the demolition of temples/structures where worship or rites are held to perpetuate the honour or memory of any individual who has committed Sati. It was thus required to create an exceptional court for hearing such cases including infringement of the law.

National Commission for Women Act 1990

The National Commission for Women Act 1990 is the pioneer in setting up National Commission for women in India. It is the statutory agency of the Indian Government made with an assumption to give guidance and ideas on arrangements influencing women. The NCW's critical target is to address women's rights and voice issues and concerns related to them in India. The settlement, governmental issues, religion, the equivalent interest of ladies in the labor force, and the treacherous working nature of women are included. The National Commission for Women is accused of researching and inspecting all matters pertinent to the sacred and other legitimate securities stood to women.

The Pre-Natal Diagnostic Techniques (Regulation and Prevention of Misuse) Act, 1994

This Act controls the usage of pre-natal characteristic methodology for the area of inherited or metabolic issues, chromosomal anomalies, certain inborn irregularities, or gender-related issues, just as the abuse of such methods for pre-natal sex assurance, which can prompt female feticide. The methods are planned to be utilized in explicit circumstances. The Act controls genetic counselling, hereditary research facilities, and hereditary centres by requiring their enlistment. But such offices are barred from publicizing pre-birth demonstrative methods for identifying or deciding the sex of the embryo. The Act makes it illicit to decide and uncover the sex of a baby to the lady or her family members. Any encroachment of this current Act's courses of action by the concerned will be punished with a fine and it will be a non-bailable offense.

Domestic Violence Act, 2005

The Domestic Violence Act of 2005 was set up to safeguard women from the heartlessness that occurs at home. This act shields women from any act/direct/oversight/commission that damages, harms, or potential to hurt are believed as oppressive conduct at home. The law is primarily intended to protect the spouse or female live-in accomplice from aggressive behavior at home executed by the spouse or male live-in accomplice or his kith and kin including sisters, widows, and moms. Abusive behavior at home is characterized as real or compromised physical, sexual, verbal, enthusiastic, or monetary maltreatment. Harassment of a lady or her relatives in the form of illegal dowry demands would also fall under these criteria. The Act attempted to address a wide range of issues that women encounter daily. It aims to provide relief to individuals who have been or are in a relationship in which one of the parties is an abuser and they have shared home through marriage, adoption, or other means. Domestic violence can take the form of actual abuse or the fear of abuse. The Act benefits women because it allows them to live in their marriage home regardless of whether they have any ownership or rights to it.

The Act is additionally significant since it prevents the victimizer to direct any further demonstrations of viciousness against ladies. The victims are protected from the attacker. The security goes up until this point that the victimizer isn't permitted to meet the lady alone and enter her work environment for interaction. The proposed Act requires the foundation of Protection Officers and non-legislative associations (NGOs) to help women with clinical assessments, legal aid, and safe asylum, in addition to other things. The Act also allows for punishment of the abuser, which might be as simple as a fine. Protection officers may be subjected to the same penalties if they fail to perform their assigned duties properly and acceptably and they might confront simple detainment as a punishment.

Child Marriage Act 2006

In October 2017, the Supreme Court of India gave over a significant choice condemning sex with a minor lady, viably finishing an exemption in Indian criminal law that had recently taken into account the culmination of marriage with an adolescent spouse. This new Act incorporates measures that deny youngster marriage, ensure and offer help to casualties, and increase the punishments for the individuals who help, advance, or solemnize such relationships. The State government is needed to assign a Child Marriage Prohibition Officer for the whole or a part of a State under this Act.

The Sexual Harassment of Women at Work Place Act 2013

The Act intends to safeguard women at work from improper conduct. Under Sections 19 and 20, the Act forces specific commitments on the employer and the District Officer like generate awareness about inappropriate behavior in the workplace; sensitize employees about the effects of the acts; helping the complaints committee in directing the examination; following up on the panel's proposals along with monitoring the well-timed submission of the advisory group's reports, in addition to other things.

1.6.3 Legal Provisions for Muslim Women

Legislations supporting Muslim Women

Muslim Personal Laws (Shariat) Act 1937

Muslim Personal Law is intended for the Muslims of India. The law talks about marriage, progression, and legacy. Everything is connected with intestate progression, the unique property of females, including individuals. Everything associated with interstate movement, the interesting property of females, including individual property gained or got under understanding or gift or another course of action of Personal Law, marriage, the breaking down of marriage, including talaq, ila, zihar, lian, khula, and Mubarak, upkeep, dower, guardianship, gifts, trusts, and trust properties, and wakfs, regardless, any customs or usage startlingly are coordinated by Muslim Personal law.

Dissolution of Muslim Marriage Act 1937

This Act passed on March 17, 1939 to allow a Muslim married woman to obtain a divorce by filing a petition against her husband, as there was previously no law allowing a wife to obtain a divorce unless her husband was impotent or imputation of unchasteness to her by her husband. Its major goal is to dispel any questions about the implications of a Muslim woman's conversion on her marriage.

Rights of Muslim women under this Act:

Unheard of: If a spouse has gone unnoticed for four years or longer, his wife may file a petition and get a decree. After six months, this goes into effect, and the marriage is dissolved. The court may not dissolve the marriage if the husband appears within these six months and agrees to fulfill marital responsibilities.

Maintenance: If a husband fails to provide for his wife for two years or more, the woman has the right to launch a lawsuit. The court may issue a decree if the wife has been living separately for two years for a reasonable reason.

Impotency: Before 1939, impotency was also a reason for divorce. This ground has been preserved in the Act.

Insanity: If the husband is insane, has leprosy, or has a venereal disease, the wife may be able to get a decree. The Act does not specify a time limit. The court will make the final decision.

Cruelty: This is a separate issue. It could be either physical or mental. Mental cruelty involves attributing unchastity and scolding repeatedly using foul terminology. The court determines what constitutes cruelty.

Imprisonment: If the husband is sentenced to seven years or more in prison and the sentence is upheld by the highest appellate court, the wife may seek a decree.

Marital responsibilities: If the husband has failed to observe marital duties for three years, the wife may obtain a decree.

The Muslim Women (Protection of Rights on Divorce) Act, 1986

The Act means to get the honors of Muslim women who are separated from husbands or are currently getting divorced from their husbands. A separated lady is entitled to all property that was given to her beforehand, during, or later the marriage by her family members or companions or by the spouse or any of the husband's family members. Furthermore, it manages upkeep instalment orders.

The Muslim Women (Protection of Rights on Marriage) Act, 2019

In reference to the Shayara Bano case, the Indian government introduced a guideline called the Muslim Women (Protection on Marriage Rights) Act, which denounces triple talaq. Any Muslim companion who expresses Talaq on their partners will be considered as a cognizable offense and will be repelled by confinement for a period that may contact three years with a fine.

1.7 Protection of Muslim women under International Instruments

Universal Declaration of Human Rights (1948):

The confirmation of the Universal Declaration of Human Rights was done in 1948. It has been announced that women are qualified for similar freedoms as a man without any kind of discrimination. The Universal Declaration was ultimately embraced with the phrasing "every single person" and "everybody" to clarify that it was expected for all kinds of people.

Convention on the Political Rights of Women (1952):

This Convention relates to ladies' political privileges drafted in 1952 and became effective on July 7, 1954. Article 1 of the convention reserves the privileges of women for casting votes in elections without any discrimination based on gender. Article 2 of the Convention complements that women are equally qualified to be chosen based on similar conditions as men without segregation. Under Article 3 of the Convention, ladies have the privilege to serve the Government in an authoritarian mode on an equal footing with men.

Declaration on the Elimination of Discrimination against Women (1967):

The said declaration is a common liberties verdict given by the General Assembly of United Nations focusing women's freedom. The declaration is designed following the features of Universal Declaration of Human Rights with an introduction and eleven articles. Unfair attitude towards women genuinely offends women's dignity under article 1 of the declaration. Article 2 of the Convention further requests the annulment of laws, customs, rules, and practices that oppress ladies. Articles 4 and 5 give ladies full discretionary privileges, including the option to cast a ballot, the capacity to look for and serve in government offices, and the opportunity to alter their nationality in the same way that males do. Article 7 states that all penal codes sections that discriminate against women must be abolished. Article 8 orders that states oppose illegal exploitation and constrained prostitution. Article 9 & 10 indicates that all suitable means needed to be guaranteed to girls and women, married and unmarried with equivalent freedoms at par with men at all levels of education, economic and public activity. Thus, public organizations, voluntary organizations and common masses are asked to uphold the functioning of the standards contained in this declaration.

Introduction

Declaration on the Protection of Women and Children in Emergency and Armed Conflict (1974):

The United Nations declaration declared to protect the vulnerable section of population like women and children amid catastrophe and guarantee their wellbeing. It asserts that the women and the children in circumstances of crisis and struggle for ensuring harmony, self-assurance, public freedom, and autonomy, ought to be given asylum, food, clinical help, and other essential privileges.

Observation of International Women's Day (8 March) & International Women's Year (1975):

Intending fully on expanding worldwide attention to women's issues, the United Nations dedicated 1975 as the year of Women's International Year in 1972. Governments, Non-profit organisations and people were approached to expand their endeavours to advance gender equality related correspondence and recognise the contribution of women towards development. The United Nations pronounced March eighth to be International Women's Day during this time. The United Nations General Assembly refers to two explanations behind observing the day is i) to understand that getting harmony and social advancement, common liberties and central opportunities, requires women's dynamic involvement, fairness, and improvement; and II) to acknowledge women's commitment to worldwide harmony and security.

Convention on the Elimination of All Forms of Discrimination against Women (CEDAW, 1979):

The Convention on the Elimination of All Forms of Discrimination Against Women, normally known as an International Bill of Rights for Women enacted by the United Nations General Assembly in 1979. The preface of the CEDAW's concedes that women face widespread discrimination and underlines such segregation mishandling the way of thinking of fairness of honors and respect for human pride. The major focal point of the convention was gender favoritism and establishing measures for countries to follow to eliminate such prejudice. States were advised to take appropriate lengths to battle a wide range of savagery occurring against ladies especially women trafficking and prostitution (Article 6) and to abolish oppression faced by women in political and public life (Art.7). Consequently, the convention settled a board on the Elimination of Discrimination against Women (CEDAW) to screen the execution part & assess its advancement.

Optional Protocol to the CEDAW:

On October 6, 1999, a discretionary convention to the CEDAW was concurred to further develop current implementation instruments for ladies' basic liberties and to raise public information on basic freedoms norms connecting with sex separation. The Optional Protocol's introduction expresses the Protocol's central goal and reason, just as the upsides of fairness and non-separation enshrined in the UDHR, CEDAW, and other worldwide basic freedoms reports.

1.8 Schemes and Policies for Welfare of Muslim Women in India

Different initiatives have been undertaken by India to empower people from all walks of life without discrimination. Women's rights, children's education, skill development, and protecting and promoting culture, particularly for minority communities, have all received special attention. Some of the measures that have been launched to empower Muslim women since 2014 include:

- Maulana Azad Educational Foundation's "Begum Hazrat Mahal National Scholarship" for Meritorious Girls (MAEF). Over 300,000 pupils from minority communities benefited from the aforementioned educational empowerment programmes between 2014 and 2018.
- National Minorities Development and Finance Corporation (NMDFC), stretches out monetary help to minorities at low pace of interest with the goal that they can begin income generating activities and become self-sustained. A measure of Rs. 19.79 billion has been received by the minority communities in concessional credits with the end goal of education and employment in 2017-18.
- The 'Nai Roshni' Scheme for Minority Women Leadership Development, which aims to empower and build confidence in women. Nearly 400 thousand women from minority populations have benefited from the programme since its start.
- Scholarship Programs: Students from ordered minority networks, like Muslims, Christians, Sikhs, Buddhists, Jains, and Parsis (Zoroastrians), who are studying in India and meet the Scheme's eligibility requirements, are eligible to apply for the scholarships.
- Telangana State Government's Shaadi Mubarak Scheme: For Muslim minorities, the Telangana State Government have launched the Shaadi Mubarak Scheme. Financial support of Rs. 51,000 (Rupees Fifty-One Thousand Only) is granted to each unmarried girl at the time of marriage under the Shaadi Mubarak Scheme. Only Telangana residents are eligible for the scheme.
- Muslim women (Protection of Rights on Marriage) Act, 2019 that annuls the act of Triple Talaq and extends gender justice and equality to Muslim women was passed by Parliament on July 30, 2019, is a huge step towards women empowerment.

1.8.1 Schemes for empowerment of Woman and Child in Assam:

The District social welfare board has adopted the following schemes for the empowerment of women and children:

i) Rajiv Gandhi Scheme for Empowerment of Adolescent Girls (SABLA)
ii) Maternity Benefit Programme (IGMSY)
iii) Homes for destitute women
iv) Beti Bachao Beti Padhao
v) One Stop Centre
vi) Women Help Line
vii) Mission Purna Shakti
viii) State Resource Centre for Women.
ix) Village Convergence and facilitation Service (VCFS)
x) Vocational Training cum Rehabilitation Centre (VTRC)

1.8.2 Schemes for the welfare of women in Cachar District

The District social welfare board has adopted the following schemes for the welfare of the women in Cachar district of Assam.

i) *Mahila Shakti Kendra:* MSK Scheme is visualized to give a point of interaction to rural women to move toward the public authority for profiting their entitlements and for enabling them through training and competence development.

ii) *Poshan Abhiyan:* It is the Government of India's lead program to work on wholesome results for children, pregnant ladies, and lactating mothers. Through the objectives, the program will endeavor to decrease the degree of under-nourishment, pallor, and low birth weight children.

iii) *Pradhan Matri Matru Vandana Yojana:* The target of the plan is i) to give partial compensation in cash to women for partial loss of wages so that sufficient rest can be given to the women earlier than and later conveyance of the primary living child. Compensation in cash would lead to further development with regards to health seeking behavior amongst the pregnant women and lactating mothers (MWCD 2017).

iv) *Ujjawala:* It is an extensive scheme meant for preventing trafficking, initiating a rescue, rehabilitation, and reintegration process for survivors of trafficking and commercial sexual exploitation. It is a comprehensive scheme of the Ministry of Women & Child Development, India.

v) *One-stop center*: The OSC offers services to all women including girls under 18 years of age affected by brutality. The objective of the program is to i) offer composing assistance to women affected by viciousness, both in private and public spaces under one roof. (ii) to give emergency and non-emergency support services including clinical, legal, mental health counseling to battle against any types of viciousness against ladies (MWCD 2017).

vi) *Swadhar Greh:* The target of the plan is to a) make available the essential need of asylums like food, clothing, clinical treatment, and care of the women in trouble; b) empower them to recover their enthusiastic strength that gets hampered because of their experience with lamentable conditions; c) furnish them with legitimate guide and direction so that they can make stride for readjustment in family/society; d) restore them financially and psychologically.

vii) *Working women hostel:* The scheme is to advance the accessibility of safe and strategically placed accommodation for working ladies with a facility of day care centers for their kids, at every possible opportunity in metropolitan, semi metropolitan or even remote regions where business opportunities for ladies exist. The hostels will be made accessible to all functioning women with no difference in class, faith, matrimonial position, and so forth. (MWCD 2015).

To summarise, domestic violence is very much prevalent in almost all cultures and religions across the globe. Causes of such violence are diverse in nature and consequences of which harms women's health and wellbeing. Considering the gravity of the issue Government of India has from time to time introduced different legislations, policies, schemes & programs, and ratified conventions to fight injustices experienced by women and uphold their rights of women of all religions. Regardless of rigid drives, women are seen to be molested, tortured, and harassed in and outside the home by intimate partners, family members, and close relatives. Hypotheses showed that various elements are related to violence against ladies and Islam's point of view mirrored that no kind of maltreatment is allowed to women in Islam. However, the number of cases is expanding, says support giving organizations of the study area. Therefore, the researcher intended to see the issue from its foundations and consequently concentrated on predominant family design, marriage, and divorce framework in Islam to get knowledge about the reasons for viciousness against women in Muslim society. The Muslim researcher and an extremist Dr. Saba Taj viewed that the pace of divorce in Muslim people in comparison to other communities is low and it was upheld by a women's wing of jaipur named all India Muslim personal law board. (India Today on April 8, 2017) and Muslim Mahila Research Kendra in light of the findings of the exploration carried out in eight districts of India by them on the issue. (The Hindu on April 10, 2017). She observed that individuals believe the polygamy marriage framework, nikah, and triple talaq just giving power to men and there is no gender balance and consequently Muslim women are getting deprived of rights. However, the course of talaq and privileges of women is obviously referenced in the heavenly Quran yet individuals need to comprehend it appropriately. She additionally stressed the point that India is facing issues like dowry, child marriage, sexual harassment, domestic violence distressing women's status across the communities. Taking into account this point, the current study laid much emphasis on conducting a review on Domestic Violence issues against Muslim Women in Cachar District of Assam. Further, to have a solid base for an in-depth analysis of the study, the researcher did a survey & review related literature. The discussion on the reviewed literature follows the next chapter.

Chapter - 2

Literature Review

The social researchers were not intense with regards to the issue of domestic violence till the second from the last quarter of the twentieth century. It was uniquely in 1970 that researchers in the west began endeavor studies to discover the nature and degree of brutality against women inside the family. They likewise directed examination to recognize the accelerating factors, which prompted abusive behavior at home against women. It was uniquely from the 1980s that disengaged endeavors were made to distinguish the idea of aggressive behavior at home against ladies. Violence against women exists similarly in the Hindu society just as in the minority networks of Muslims, Christians or Sikhs said Bano, 1989 in her discussion on Violence on Women in Muslim Society: the Case of Divorced Women held in context to divorce and violence. A significant part of the current writing on the Muslim ladies in India is restricted to a thought of their status and job with regards to Islam and its effect on them. All religions have concurred ladies a mediocre status and consigned them to an optional position. Nonetheless, religion itself is the result of man-centric culture and unless these essential cultural qualities change, women will keep on experiencing a circumstance where religion and man-centric culture are in union. In this section through thematic reviews i) Women & Violence; ii) Domestic Violence against Muslim Women (National & International Perspective); iii) Factors causing brutality at home against Muslim Women; iv) Affects of Domestic Violence; v) Help-seeking behaviour of Muslim women; v) Measures adopted for eliminating Domestic violence an attempt has been made to gain a better understanding on the stated problem.

Women and Violence

Davis J. Nanette (1988) stated that domestic violence occurs in intimate relations within the households and conjugal assault, the danger for homicide, torment, and provocation slapping, gnawing and hitting constituting women battering.

The result of an observational review directed in 4 urban areas of Rajasthan viz. Jaipur, Ajmer, Kota, and Udaipur by Ahuja (1998) on viciousness against women uncovered that it is comparatively normal to ladies that have a place with families that are all the more patriarchally coordinated. All types of savagery against ladies have all the earmarks of being higher in lower financial layers, however, guilty parties are not really from lower classes. The larger part of the occurrences shows up against ladies who need monetary assets. Young ladies were the most noticeably awful victim of brutality. Countless ladies who are casualties of brutality are the individuals who need self-assurance, have helpless mental self-portrait and a sensation of defencelessness, and have a couple of social ties, companionships, or local area affiliations. Further, the review uncovers that viciousness against ladies isn't the after effect of their provocative conduct but instead the consequence of the guilty party's learned social reactions. The culprits of brutality are not drunkards and mental cases who come from disrupted families yet are ordinary guys. The investigation discovered that police response to female survivors of viciousness is by and large apathetic and negative rather than accommodating and agreeable. Response of relatives to casualties of brutality is preferably uncaring over thoughtful. Further, the course of recuperation by the casualty post-quake tremor depends both on her character qualities just as on the construction of circumstance wherein she resides and works.

Rastoi and Paul Therly (2006) tried to comprehend the connection between dowry and viciousness against women. The author saw that generally in the event of an organized marriage, exchange concerning the transfer of resources for the groom happens for marrying the bride. If the amount of dowry dissatisfies the groom and his family then it leads to violence against women. Sometimes dissatisfaction accentuates dowry deaths or the women put to death by her husband and his families.

Qureshi (2007) in his study on Women and Crime in India reveals that women are victims of both structural and behavioral violence. He has interviewed 30 women of the upper, middle, and lower classes (10 from each group) to get some idea of their victimization. The educational status of the respondents reveals that upper and middle-class women are better in terms of education than the lower-class women group. However, women from each group are victims of violence in different forms.

Simister, J. (2008) concentrated on abusive behavior at home among a couple in India. This paper centersaround violence by spouses against wives, overlooking different sorts of viciousness. The author visualizes that violence is less in the case of educated couples. Prioritization of schooling for young ladies and young men has been given emphasis by the author.

Suresh Goel (2009) expressed that aggressive behavior at home is a coercive disposition towards someone includes terrorizing, undermining, badgering the victim. He additionally referenced that abusive behavior at home incorporates physical, sexual, passionate, and mental maltreatment. Giving a lot of significance to the detached maltreatment of the person in question, the creator clarifies that 'inactive maltreatment is secretive and hidden which incorporates exploitation, equivocalness, and disregard profound and scholarly maltreatment'.

Alice Edwards (2011) fundamentally looks at how women live, perceive, and react in a situation when they face viciousness from a human rights perspective. The study highlighted that the two main approaches have been adopted by the international human rights bodies to address the issue like i) to create an impression that violence against women is a type of gender discrimination and ii) innovatively rework on existing common freedoms arrangements so that it can be applied as per the need and violence experiences of women. The author suggested focusing on the right to life as an approach to get liberated from torment and other horrible, barbaric, or debasing treatment or discipline.

Rinki Bhattacharjee (2013) expressed that, it is the most demeaning experience for women to be attacked and assaulted by an extremely intimate individual like spouse and incalculable women of each culture of India are encountering such harmful conduct on regular basis. The author highlighted that the voices of women always remain unheard when the question of violence against them comes.

Sex is a weapon utilized by the husband upon his better half mercilessly and it becomes a significant element for abusive behavior at home against women says, Vandana (2017). In India, the idea of conjugal assault has not yet been recognized but is widely approved in erstwhile countries. As indicated by her, the essential justification behind a lady to tolerate such maltreatment is to just maintain the family integrity. The women victims believe that sex is a private matter which ought not to be talked about in the open otherwise this may dismal the family reputation and integrity which in other ways prevent many women from seeking help from many support providing agencies.

Sharma P. and Khokhar A. (2021) directed a study to discover the prevalence of aggressive behavior at home and adapting systems among wedded grown-ups during COVID pandemic induced lockdown in India. It was a cross-sectional study led among married people in April 2020. The study could capture the responses of 94 respondents; around 7.4% had confronted abusive behaviour at home during the lockdown. Of these 7 members, around 85.7% announced expanded recurrence of aggressive behaviour at home during the lockdown. Most of the victims decided to overlook it (57.1%), or utilized yoga/contemplation (42.9%) to adapt.

Sahayak (2021) viewed that in Islam polygamy is practiced with or without the permission of the first wife. Wives who are financially dependent on their husbands find it difficult to show denial towards husbands' will to marry again. This is one of the reasons why wives are hesitant to go for divorce knowing the fact that the husband is violating the marriage contract.

Muslim Women and Domestic Violence

A study conducted by Babu and Kar (2009) on domestic violence against women in Eastern India covered both wedded women and men respondents from three of the four territories of Eastern India. The study observed that husband and their parents were involved in abusing wives and daughter in law at home. But in maximum cases, it was the husband who was found involved in abusing the wife at home.

Bhatti, et al., (2011) conducted a study to understand how women are surviving against domestic violence in district Jacobabad Sindh in Pakistan. The study showed that women getting married at an early age were deprived of their basic rights and faced the biggest challenges. Their mobility is restricted by their husbands. Drawing out the old information into the setting of the study, the author mentioned that in the initial six months of the year 1992, the district recorded cases of stove burn from almost 500 women and 370 cases of killing. The specialists at the Burn Unit of one of the presumed emergency clinics of Pakistan assessed that around 60% of ladies have been signed by their spouses or parents-in-law.

A. R. F. Begum (2014) carried out a study on Srilankan Muslim women's experience towards aggressive behavior at home. The study explored that Muslim ladies are victims of several types of cruelty, particularly by their husbands. Wives should take permission for everything from husbands. Women were not allowed to contact their friends or family members without the permission of the husband. Women were emotionally abused by husbands by threatening to remarry. They are also fettled bysexual abuse and economic abuse. The study also reflected that Muslim women are not coming up with their problems. They consider it as a personal problem and a dispute between husband and wife so instead of disclosing it prefers to keep the matter private.

Niu and Laidler (2015) studied the harmful encounters of Hui Muslim ladies in China. For the study, fourteen Muslim women of west China having experience of encountering domestic violence have been interviewed and the findings reflected that low socio-economic status & minority ethnic character made Hui women vulnerable to domestic violence. But a constant fear of being overlooked, segregated, marginalization increased women's patience towards cruelty. It shows Hui women are frail as well as impervious to viciousness. They are reconciling themselves under controlled mechanisms of society and underlying imbalances uncover their independence and insight.

Kozieł, P. (2017) investigated the problems encountered by Muslim and Christian women in gender-based violence. It has also examined the rights of women under Sharia in Northern Nigeria. From a gender and anthropological perspective, the current state of ladies in Nigeria reflects their unsteadiness and negligence against the context-oriented foundation in which sex-based savagery meets with political-strict insurrection. The review referenced that thousands of ladies were kidnapped in Northern Nigeria since 2014. In every three women, one aged between 15-24 years in Nigeria is a survivor of brutality. However, these records are not being reported because of socio-psychological factors.

Aliakbari et al., (2018) conducted population-based research on 400 Iranian Women to understand the level of domestic violence among them. The study indicated that the severity of the domestic violence was 54%. Among the others the most commonly found violence was physical, mental and sexual (41.4%). It was also observed that 30.8% women expressed about having sex without their consent and they used to be slapped (25.7%). A complicated couple relationship was noticed by the author in the study.

Ahmad, S. M. (2019) in his study presented a narrative of Islamophobic brutality as a sort of sex-based viciousness that happens with Canadian Muslim women. The study interviewed 21 Muslim ladies in Toronto and encompassed regions to address their experiences with Islamophobic viciousness. Altogether 30 women have participated in the study. The investigation explored that violence incorporates attacks on the body; sexual & verbal battering. All events of physical and sexual ruthlessness uncovered by members were said to have been executed by white men. Numerous respondents viewed that they were made targeted because of the Islamophobic brutality. Islamophobic dialogue presents Muslim women as being inactive, feeble easily making Muslim women victims of domestic violence. Surprisingly, out of 30, only three respondents approached police for support.

A study conducted by Isgandarova, N. (2017) on the issue of aggressive behaviour at home executed upon the expectant ladies in Azerbaijani aiming to know how far the ideologies of Islam supported expectant women victim of brutality to resolve the issues related to brutality against them. The outcome proposes that aggressive behavior at home against pregnant ladies is altogether decreased during pregnancy. The author viewed that a few social and strict elements assume a critical part in lessening or expanding the frequency of savagery against pregnant ladies. For instance, the Azerbaijani government of late has taken a few measures to handle brutality against ladies. Nonetheless, applying moderate Islamic lessons can build the morale of such initiatives taken for handling domestic violence against expecting ladies in the study area.

The author examined how the marginalisation of the Muslims in India and the United Kingdom led sex based violence in Muslim communities. For the study the authors Chantler, K., et al., (2019) initially outlined communalism in India and radicalization in Europe and furthermore did a review on laws considering individual laws of India and the call to Shariah law in the UK to understand by which these policies, laws, and dialogues affect Muslim women encountering GVB in both the settings. Authors presume that there is a gamut between state reactions and local area reactions with regards to law embedded with gender based violence at an underlying and relational stage in India & Europe and the current socio-political setting additionally endpoints community places available to Muslim women to get to help for GBV.

The author tried to understand the violence related experience of women working as frontline service providers from their close partners, Milani, A., et al., (2018). Respondents based on their knowledge of the issue and practical experiences shared the factors causing violence in intimate relationships. According to them authoritarian culture, male dominance, Immigration, belief, socialist thinking, are the significant subjects of violence.

The paper explores the peculiarity of brutality against ladies in the Ghanaian Muslim community. To begin with, the paper gives a theological impression of Quranic texts and raises the issue of interpretation/misinterpretation and the degree to which religion has assumed a basic part in endorsing brutality against Muslim ladies. Author Ammah, R. (2009) further inspect how Muslim ladies in Ghana have soaked up these tests through socialization and obliviousness. Second, it talks about how equal perusing of the text can be utilized as religious assets for developing the condition of Muslim ladies with the different avenues accessible for equalizing the women's status and proposed recommendations to control the occurrence of violence.

Factors influencing Domestic Violence against Muslim Women

According to Njenga (1999) the monetary weakness of men is one of the reasons for abusive behavior at home. The men, who fail to establish authority mentally or monetarily, tend to exercise power physically.

Ondicho (2000) focuses on the reasons for aggressive behavior at home and explores the lawful encounters of battered women and their discernment about Domestic viciousness in Nairobi. The study discovered that the explanation of abusive behavior at home isn't restricted to a specific religion, age, ethnic gathering, or social class. The author is of the assessment that abusive behaviour at home against women is considered to be an element of man-centric authoritarian structure inside the family, where men are better than women and the women are men's ownership to be treated as they wish and consider proper. The financial reliance of women on men is the primary justification behind which ladies don't leave their husbands or make any lawful move against them. It was likewise observed that a larger part of the ladies casualties stayed in their connections with their batterers because of financial reliance on their accomplices and absence of choices work or outside the relationship.

INCLEAN (2000) tracked down aggressive behavior at home as an issue that continues across age, social class, and religion in India. The study is of the view that 40% of ladies had encountered no less than one type of actual brutality in their wedded life. Gerstein (2000) expressed that low instructive levels and poverty are significant purposes behind aggressive behavior at home. Further, marriage at a more youthful age makes women powerless against abusive behavior at home (Mishra, 2000; Hindin, 2002 and Rao, 1997). Sahu, 2003 argued that socialization with regards to sexual orientation has a connection with violence and the socialization process is liable for abusive behavior at home against women.

Sharifa Alkhateeb (2004) expressed that an authoritarian family structure is responsible for making American Muslims abused in one way or other and conceivably make people causalities of brutality. Generally, women and child is abused because of the dominant characteristics of the husbands. The father socializes his wife and children in such a way so that they start believing and realizing that whatever he wants family will have to do the same and it is the same as what Allah wants him to do.

A study on Muslim Women conducted by Hasan and Menon (2004) revealed that around 20% of respondents had encountered verbal and actual maltreatment in the conjugal home, more than 80% of it on account of their spouses. The drinking propensity of the spouse, husbands going out without telling their wives, and sharing of property were found as the fundamental driver of aggressive behavior at home against women. The women have expressed that in any case, Purdah is not a reason for making them victim of abusive behaviour at home.

Choudhary, R. et al., (2006) observed that utilization of liquor by the spouse was viewed as a significant reason for abusive behavior at home against women. The review uncovers that Domestic violence is in existence in the Indian culture and women are exceptionally not much aware about the legislations & associations managing aggressive behavior at home. The review showed that liquor addiction of spouses is one of the primary drivers of aggressive behavior at home against ladies.

Salarifar, M. R. (2009) conducted a study intending to comprehend the reasons for domestic violence against women of Iran.The result mirrored that the reasons for domestic violence are confined to personal, interpersonal, and social factors. Problems related to physical inability, hormonal issues of males have been considered as the personal issue for which violence at home is taking place. Causes like sex, social learning, and relational problems have been considered as interpersonal problems causing violence at home. Unemployment, low income, judgemental attitude towards women are the social factors that cause violence at home.

Gaikwad (2011) attempted to understand the relationship between sexually transmitted diseases with abusive behavior at home. The study was conducted with 76 respondents of Bangalore. Findings revealed that none of the respondents reported to the police. Further, the review investigated that the abusive behavior against women is associated with the age of marriage of women, the duration of the marriage, and the alcoholic nature of husbands.

A cross-sectional study was conducted by Dalal, K., and Lindqvist, K. (2012) with 124385 respondents constituting with weeded women of regenerative age groups of 29 states of India. The investigation discovered that working positions, poor economic conditions of women, and domineering conduct of husbands appeared as sturdy forecasters of violence at homes in India. The women victims had experienced the violence of different forms in their lifetime. Of which 14% were the victims of emotional abuse; less severe physical abuse was experienced by 31% of the victims & 10% of the victims have severely encountered physical abuse and only 8% were abused sexually. Ladies belonging to scheduled castes and Islam religion were found to be more exposed to domestic violence.

A qualitative study led by Khatri and Pandey (2013) saw that violence against women has developed as an arrangement of gender-based relations that brings up the notion that men are better than women. According to the authors, Ignorance and monetary reliance over males were fundamental variables of violence, helpless access in dynamic force of ladies, early marriage, conventional convictions, values, standards which were well established to brutality against ladies. Mental torment, disregard, and actual beating were the most well-known causes of brutality. Conjugal assault and lewd behavior were likewise found sometimes. The culprits were spouses trailed by parents-in-law. Utilization of liquor, the matchless quality sensation of men, spouses' propensity for paying attention to other relatives, betting, sexual disappointment were the fundamental purposes behind the brutality against ladies. Alongside, joblessness of the respondents, extra-marital undertakings, & child inclination within the relations were likewise considered the reasons of viciousness against women.

Muhuya, R. K. (2013) made a study on domestic violence in the Cachar District from a human rights perspective. The significant focus of the study was to analyze the role of national and international instruments meant for the protection of human rights of women; to comprehend the nature and types of aggressive behavior at home; the reaction of the victims towards aggressive behavior at home; to look at the awareness level of the victims towards legal redressal mechanisms. The fundamental reasons for aggressive behavior at home found in the review are extramarital issues of the spouse, husband wants to get remarried, and inability to bring settlement articles during and after marriage, and so forth which affected most of the victims physically followed by verbal abuse by their better half and parents in law.

Tenkorang, E. Y. et al., (2013) carried out a study in Ghana on the issues related to violence affecting women at home to find the purposes behind both physical and sexual fierceness among married women in Ghana. A total of 1835 married women of the age group of 15-45 years have participated in the study. The finding reveals that the low level of education of women was the fundamental driver of both physical and sexual viciousness among the women of Ghana. Women who found wife-beating justified those women expressed about controlled nature of husbands and thus had higher possibilities of experiencing physical & sexual viciousness.

An investigation on the causes of viciousness among the Thai Muslim married couples in Satun Province presented that suspicious and jealous attitude of the husband; drug abuse and alcoholic nature; lack of mental and physical preparedness for their own family; lack of contribution in family work; belief in male dominance by the husband are the precipitating factors of domestic violence (Laeheem, K. 2014). The author suggested different approaches for dealing with such factors separately. To trim down jealousy and suspicious attitude, the author suggested maintaining transparency and consistency with each other. In accordance to the researcher, if the husbands are religious, the possibility of creating violence against women especially for the habit of drinking and abusing drugs will decrease. In this direction, Islamic leaders and religious organizations may work for promoting knowledge of religious principles to make Thai families understand faith, practice, and morals. Married couples should be aware of their roles in a marital relationship and the activities that make the family happy. Even before marriage both the partners can undergo a training program on happy families endorsed by the Provincial Islamic Committee. Even the leaders and organizations may focus to eradicate the concept of male dominance over females from Thai society and to lay importance on promoting values, human rights, and equality in the society.

Sarma, B. B. (2014) tried to discover the current circumstance of women in India as compared to the advancement of the world scenario. The review uncovers that the breakdown of the joint family system is one of the reasons of abusive behavior at home in India which deprives young couples of getting legitimate direction and guidance. Moreover, reasons like control and access love to recently weeded women; control and love to recently wedded ladies, spouse rules their better half and not gave authorization to taking care of business, a couple questioning each other for extra conjugal undertakings, Alcoholic nature and drinking propensities for the husband and so on. The author proposed a few arrangements like the GOs and NGOs should endeavor to beat this major issue of the general public, the networks should uphold the casualties of DV, sexual orientation refinement program ought to advance in the instructive foundations and so on. The exploration ought to follow a solid support exertion towards organizing ladies' common freedoms.

S. Priscila Sharon (2014) communicated that aggressive behavior at home is not just goals physical and mental maltreatment rather it incorporates battering, sexual maltreatment of young lady & youngsters in the household, dowry-related viciousness, conjugal assault, female genital mutilation. The author expressed that consumerist culture has just contributed to the progression of barbarities, brutality, and actual attacks against ladies.

Banashree (2015) did a study in the Tinsukia district of Assam intending to discover the reasons for abusive behavior at home against women and to concentrate on the effect of abusive behavior at home to the victim women, their kids and their family relations. An example of 100 families having a place with various financial statuses from provincial areas of Tinsukia District was arbitrarily chosen. The alcoholic nature of the spouse was the significant explanation of aggressive behavior at home. However, the information uncovered that in all cases aggressive behavior at home was caused not due to a solitary explanation. In the enormous number of cases, a blend of various causes was noticed. The aggressive behavior at home additionally impacted the physical and emotional wellness of the victim in various ways.

Wrang L. (2016) attempted to understand the factors influencing attitude towards intimate partner violence (IPV). A few variables including age, sexual orientation, education, residency, financial status, man-centric role, etc. impact the attitude concerning IPV. Of which schooling may be the most critical one because age, sex, gender role are reflected in distinctive instructional level and factors such as financial status, taking part in family choice, capacity to get to media, and man-centric sexual orientation are embedded in education. The study suggested that further population-based research may offer more clear knowledge into factors affecting attitude in regards to IPV and more exertion of government in advancing people's schooling is required.

A study led by AnuradhaNadda (2018) on 'Aggressive behavior at home among currently Married Females of Haryana, India', introduced the viciousness experienced by the women of Haryana. The state recorded 28% viciousness among wedded ladies when contrasted with the public figure which was 39.7%. The predominance of aggressive behavior at home in rural and metropolitan spaces of Haryana was viewed as 29.1% and 25.3% separately, contrasted with the public figures of 38.3% and 29.4% individually. The review investigated that rural women are more helpless against aggressive behavior at home than metropolitan women because of their low degree of education, pay, awareness, privileges.

A study conducted in West Iran by Afkhamzadeh, A. et al., (2019) with a purpose to review the prevalence of abusive behaviour at home with its connected variables in Sanandaj district of Iran. The respondent for the study was 360 women. The significant discoveries of the review mirrored that the prevalence of violence was 71% in the past year and specifically the occurrence of emotional, sexual, and physical brutality was 62.2%, 48.7% & 49.9% respectively. The study shared that any type of brutality has a huge relationship with women's profession, the financial status of a family, the situation with sexual fulfillment of couples. The pervasiveness of abusive behavior at home against women is high and disturbing in Sanandaj, Iran. Given the connection between the experience of violence and sexual disappointment; sexual education when marriage is suggested for couples. It is also suggested that screening programs can be organized to identify the victims of domestic violence. Thus, couples who have hazard variables will be guided with the required measures.

Gama A. et al., (2021) analyzes the event of abusive behavior at home, related factors, and help-seeking behavior during the COVID-19 pandemic. The study found that married women of lower age groups are more vulnerable to abusive behavior at home. Most of the respondents' victims didn't look for help, the principal reasons being thinking about it superfluous, that help would not transform anything, and having a humiliating outlook on what had occurred. Just 4.3% of the casualties looked for police help. The most widely recognized purposes behind not approaching to shape a grievance were thinking about the maltreatment was not serious and accepting the police would do nothing.

Effects of Domestic Violence on Muslim Women

RavneetK., and Suneela G. (2008) featured the impacts of aggressive behavior at home. The author referenced that aggressive behavior at home not only causes physical injuries but also harms a victimized woman socially, economically, emotionally, psychologically, spiritually and society as a whole and truly affects women's reproductive and sexual wellbeing.

Saghiret.et al., (2011) in their review named Gender and Violence: A Rising Issue observed that brutality has various structures, for example, physical, verbal, versatility, mental, social, and financial which affects women at various stages of life. The author suggested Government, Government, scholars, and associations should play their part in putting such practices down.

Shahzadi, N. K., et al., (2012) surveyed 100 Muslim women in Pakistan aiming to know how abusive behavior at home is affecting women's psychology. The study found that limited movement at the societal level affects Muslim women's education and work opportunities which affect women more psychologically than physically. It puts women with numerous mental turmoil like depression, anxiety, suicide, drug addiction which further calls for psychological medical treatment in Pakistan. The author suggested that more awareness of women's education and women's rights is the need of the hour for Pakistan and an immense role can be played by Government and Non-Government Organisations in the said aspects by making provisions for women's education and employment.

Prescila (2014) keeps up that viciousness against women in India is an issue of cultural standards and monetary reliance. Female feticide, lewd behavior, and different types of sexual orientation-based brutality comprise the truth of most young girls' and womens' lives in India. Spouse battering influences the physical and mental prosperity of abused women and their children too. Though the participation of women is increasing in the public sphere and laws are amended as per the need and requirement yet India has quite far to go to make Indian women equivalent residents in their own country itself. Numerous ladies are fiercely treated by their partners and they experience peacefully. In certain situations, aggressive behavior at home prompts the passing of these women.

Elizabeth Gabriel (2015) investigated the nature, causative factors, and effects of Domestic Violence and also measured the level of stress, coping methods, help-seeking behaviors, and the awareness of victims regarding the services available for protection of women from domestic violence. Physical, Psychological, social, and economic effects were found in all aspects of the respondents. The level of stress was also found to be present in all three categories namely physical, psychological and behavioral. 87.75% of the respondents had medium levels of stress effects in them due to domestic violence. The hypothesis test results showed that the factors such as verbal abuse and emotional abuse got a significant level of difference in the stress level of the respondents. But factors such as physical violence, financial abuse, and sexual abuse have no significant level of difference made in stress levels. It was also found out that there exists a significant difference between stress and the type of family of the respondents. In addition to all these, the effects which are latent and those which can't be expressed by words seemed to be much more.

Rajkumari, et al., (2016) assessed the extent and the elements associated with aggressive behavior at home among married women of 18 to 49 years availed outdoor health services from a hospital based at Imphal, Manipur during February and March 2015. It was found in the study that the greater part of the respondents 278(53.6%) have confronted some type of brutality during their conjugal life. Verbal type of savagery 218(78.4%) was the commonest followed by actual brutality 134(48.2%). The study addressed that viciousness was significantly connected with the number of kids, smoking, and alcoholic nature of husband. A greater part of the women (54.5%) was monetarily reliant upon their mate. The most widely recognized reason for viciousness (41.4%) as detailed was 'Contentions because of monetary issue'. The author viewed that monetary reliance and less education of women are the two major influencing factors for violence. Investigations discovered that women having higher monetary status are in a better position to change conventional gender roles. It has been accounted that elevated levels of schooling for men and women would decrease the violence rate. A considerable number of the respondents conceded that they had experienced physical viciousness which required clinical consideration yet the vast majority of them didn't report the episode dreading social shame and further exploitation by relatives.

A study conducted by Ashraful, I. L. (2016) in Barak Valley of Assam aimed to comprehend the structures and reasons for brutality against Muslim women. The consequence of the review uncovers that a greater part of the casualties is manhandled genuinely which is trailed by mental and sexual maltreatment.

Terra Pingley (2017) looked into some past research works that reviewed the experiences of youths who witness forceful conduct at home and its impacts on their practices, changes, and improvement. Accordingly a survey has been conducted to investigate the inquiry like: What is the effect of abusive behavior at home on children? The findings show that children are very much exposed to domestic violence and intimate partner violence which is going to affect them in their holistic development. Under this backdrop, the study emphasized that identifying the effects of violence at home should be identified and dealt with diligently.

Carolin, P.A and G. Gladston, X. G. (2020) discussed different parts of aggressive behavior at home and its effect on kids. Abusive behavior at home is a worldwide issue of huge extents. It can likewise be called private accomplice brutality which happens between individuals in any close connection. It takes various structures including passionate, sexual, actual maltreatment, and dangers of misuse. An unevenness of force and control will forever be engaged with an oppressive relationship. Worldwide assessments published by WHO demonstrate that in 3(35%) of ladies globally have encountered either physical or sexual intimate partner viciousness. Authors viewed that children who are presented to brutality in their homes may become the victim of physical maltreatment which will create a long haul physical and psychological wellness issue. Children are the weak group who can be taken advantage of and mishandled in various structures. Surprisingly, in most cases, they are mishandled inside their own home by their people.

Alharbi F. et al., (2021) conducted an empirical study in Saudi Arabia with an objective to understand violence scenarios from a pre and during pandemic perspective. An aggregate, of 2254 members were interviewed for the study. The findings reflected that the prevalence of aggressive behavior at home before the COVID 19 pandemic was 25.4% and 16.6% during COVID 19 restrictions. Before COVID 19, instances of grown maltreatment and forceful conduct between Saudi wedded couples were expanding every year which became a subject of concern both socio-therapeutically. But with the constrained in-house imprisonment initiative as a part of regulatory approach showed a general abatement of 8.8% in the declared cases.

Help seeking behaviour of Muslim Women victims of Domestic Violence

The review presents the extent of physical savagery by spouses, its exposure, and the assistance-looking attitude of abused ladies belonging to both rural and urban areas of Bangladesh. For the study, the author interviewed 28 wedded ladies who were truly manhandled by their spouses. Findings showed that physical spousal violence was prevalent among 40% women of in urban areas and 42% among rural women. A larger portion i.e. 66% mishandled women were quiet with regards to their experience. The primary explanations for this quiet were a high acknowledgment of brutality, shame, and anxiety toward more prominent damage. The author Naved, R. T. et al., (2006) explored that 60% of women victims of urban areas and 51% victims of rural areas never received any assistance from others. Just 2% of women sought help from different institutions when they failed to bear the sufferings any longer the violence became dangerous and the children were in danger. The author viewed that facilitating the victims with needed services is necessary; at the same time encouraging the utilization for such services is similarly important to expand help towards individuals for conquering the obstructions looked by them while accessing such services.

Schuler, S. R. et al., (2008) conducted a study on the rights of women, violence at home, and help to seek in Rural Bangladesh. The author reported that a blend of poverty, sex imbalance, disparities in the legitimate structure, male-centric mentalities, and debasement in both formal and casual establishments deter abused women of Rural Bangladesh from seeking help and lessening the probability of a good result when they approach.

The author through a study analyzed the relationship between types, severity & duration of violence caused by an intimate partner and victims' approaches towards availing medical and legal services. For this purpose, data has been collected from 1509 respondents. The study presented that women with sexual abuse were more in seeking medical care in comparison to women with psychological abuse. Further, women experienced with physical violence by intimate partners were 3.2 times more than women victims of sexual violence by intimate mate partners (1.6 times) who sought legal services. The seriousness of the violence has increased the help clinical and legitimate assistance looking seeking among the victims. Seeking medical help increased among sexually abused women and legal help among physically abused women. The study showed that there is a clear association between sexual and physical intimate partner violence and legal help-seeking.

The study conducted by Kar (2009) examined the worldwide situation of domestic violence and Indian circumstance on Domestic Violence. The author keeps up with that in India there are sufficient legislations to shield ladies from abusive behavior at home but fails when the question of execution in a significant manner comes into practice.

Pathak, B. (2009) in her study on Domestic Violence: Need for Social Awareness opines that the domestic violence act 2005 meant for the protection of women has legally strengthened women's position in India but in practice, women are the worst sufferer of domestic violence due to low awareness of laws and other protective measures for women. The author emphasizes the need for social awareness which will enable people to be legally conscious. Further, women's empowerment is necessary for ensuring not just their protection and welfare, but the well-being of the entire family.

An observational study has been conducted to understand the consequences of domestic violence along with the measures considered to control the abusive behavior against women at home by Choudhury R. et al., (2014). The study indicated that liquor addiction is the principal reason for the brutality against women and to combat such issues socio-legal support services were made available to the victims. But due to a lack of awareness about mentioned services, the victims could not reap the benefit.

This study looks at the financial attributions that convince an abused woman in India either to stay quiet or come close to someone for seeking help to respond to the harmful conduct at home. The financial condition of victims decides the decision of choosing formal and casual organizations for looking for help. The result of the review recommends that academic position along with monetary status have an imperative influence in deciding whether to search for help to stop harmful conduct at home or not. However, the study found that informal means of seeking help are widely accepted than formal sources.

A study directed by Leonardsson, M., and San Sebastian, M. (2017) a target to analyze the pervasiveness and indicators of help-seeking among ladies in India who are the casualties of various types of spousal viciousness. For the cross-sectional review information has been gathered from 19,125 respondents constituting married isolated, separated and bereaved ladies in India who experienced physical or sexual viciousness by their spouses were acquired from National Family Health Survey III 2005-2006. Investigation reveals that only (23.7%) of them had encountered some type of spousal brutality and looked for help. However, only 1% had looked for help from formal sources. For women who had encountered physical, sexual, and psychological savagery together, help-seeking behavior is prevalent among them (48.8%) and it is seen least in the ladies who were only exposed to sexual brutality (1.5%). The indicator behind seeking help was the injury caused by serious brutality. It is seen in the study that women of North and North East and the women with kids were less inclined to seek help.

The author opined that many women who experienced intimate partner violence do not report their cases to the domestic violence and victim support unit (a department of Ghana police services), Ghana. The study analyzed challenges associated with help-seeking at DOVVSU with data from 565 Ghanian female victims of IPV. Results demonstrated that a significant number of respondents could not say whether police headquarters in their locality had DOVVSU units or not. The people who didn't know were fundamentally less inclined to look for help than the individuals who had some awareness of the assistance. Ladies who saw 'disgrace' and 'monetary limitations' as obstructions were essentially less inclined to report or look for help at DOVVSU. The individuals who believed the police sought help from DOVVSU than the people who didn't. Contrasted with those with no education, highly educated women had higher chances of looking for help from DOVVSU. The study findings proposed the need to work on the perceivability of DOVVSU and to escalate education on intimate partner violence. Additionally Ghanian Govt. ought to expedite the fund to fight domestic violence issues to support those women who don't come forward for help-seeking because of monetary reasons.

A study was undertaken by Sepali G. et al., (2021) in Canada highlighted the risk factors that were associated with domestic violence during the pandemic. In response Government of Canada has taken many approaches for reducing the impact of infection. Among which mental health services to the victims helped the person concerned and family to minimize the effects of domestic violence.

Emerging reactions carried out to forestall and react to savagery against women and kids in WHO European part states during the COVID-19 pandemic: a perusing survey of online media reports, Pearson S. et al., (2021). The study aimed to understand the approaches adopted by Government and Non-Government organizations to check and react to the rise of violence against women during the 2019 Covid pandemic. This review uncovers that in 52 of the 53 part states there was somewhere around one measure attempted to forestall brutality against ladies during the pandemic. Government-drove or government-supported measures were the most well-known. Non-administrative and other common society-drove anticipation and reaction measures were accounted for in 40 part states. The most widely recognized measure was the utilization of media and web-based media to bring issues to light on brutality against ladies and to offer types of assistance through internet-based stages, trailed by measures taken to extend helpline administrations for those presented to violence.

Measures to eliminate violence against Muslim women

Michau, L. (2007) citing the role performed by Uganda-based NGOs on domestic violence issues, said that the NGOs can raise voices for exploring community-based domestic violence prevention methodologies to curb the attitudes and behaviors of perpetrators of domestic violence. The primary prevention efforts at the community level would yield meaningful results so far eradication of violence against women is concerned. Therefore, the author argues that community mobilization is essential to bring sustainable change on the issue of violence against women

Laskar, N. H. (2014) in his study on "Violence against Women: Female Foeticide and Infanticide" finds that female infanticide is more in lower classes whereas foeticide is prevalent among the middle and upper classes. He maintains that women education economic employment, realizing their strength in social situation, economic and political empowerment is essential for raising their status in society.He further focuses on the responsibility of society to create human rights atmosphere and violation-free society for women.

Prabodh, K. G. (2014) underscored the earnest need of taking on the Uniform Civil Code in India. He viewed that the degree and nature of Article 44 have been totally misjudged. It doesn't examine a solitary normal common code rather it discusses uniform common code which may be a lot of various other common codes focused on different networks.

Rawal, P. and Singh, J. (2014) conducted a review on the Practice of Dowry and Domestic Violence. The author studied forty instances of dowry-related aggressive behavior at home in western UP, India. Findings presented that most of the women 52.5% experienced dowry-related forceful conduct at home. 55% of women belonged to a family with lower economic conditions and 92.5% of women are not working. 55% reported early marriages cases and represented lower educational status. The study suggested that economic reinforcement, alongside high-level education and changed social norms may safeguard ladies from such sort of social evils.

Dhirendra, K.J., and Shyam, S. A. (2014) conducted a study in Balasore district aiming to understand abusive behavior from a human rights perspective. The author observed in his studies that Muslim and tribal ladies lack awareness about their basic liberties which put them in difficult circumstances and confront with instances of infringement in and outside the home. The study recommended that proper education and awareness should be the approach to curb violence against women. The study further suggested the involvement of Self-help groups, non-government organizations, civil societies, community-based organizations in looking at the issue diligently and taking initiatives for its eradication.

Chowdhury, M.A.K. (2015) completed a review in Bangladesh with a target to distinguish the reasons for abusive behavior at home against ladies of various socio-social foundation and emphasised legitimate point of view over the circumstance in Bangladesh. The study uncovers that aggressive behavior at home against ladies in Bangladesh is lawful, monetary, instructive, formative and basic liberties issue.It was suggested by the author that the diverse methodologies ought to be intended for execution of the current law of the nation in regards to the abusive behavior at home against women; alongside awareness should be raised among individuals to make the laws socially considerable; and to urge victims for registering their complaints. Along these lines, the public authority and the non-government organisations (NGOs) should cooperate to make the general public more tranquil and brutal free.

The study by Jennifer et al., (2016) focused on the alcohol use of the husband; violence by the intimate partner and maltreatment by the family members to the pregnant women in Mumbai. For the study, the authors interviewed 1,038 post-pregnancy women. The investigation showed that the drinking habit of the husband is a serious threatening factor for intimate partner violence in post-pregnancy phase of women. The study suggested that there is a need to increase demonstrated effective mediations for decreasing men's liquor use and plan methodologies that give ladies security from liquor-related IPV.

World health organization (2020) viewed that containing pandemic-induced violence at home may cause long-term effects. Thus dynamic measures towards reconnaissance and management of domestic violence should be a crucial piece of a battle against COVID-19.

Violence against Women during COVID-19 Restrictions by Elisabeth R. et al., (2020) uncovers expanded family pressure and intimate partner brutality. The author recommended that the health providers ought to know about the dangers and outcomes of violence against women and furnish those impacted with help and significant clinical treatment. It is vital to guarantee the support of fundamental clinical benefits, for example, post-assault care, including the accessibility of the essential medications and different supplies. More seasoned ladies, ladies with handicaps, ladies living in compassionate emergencies settings, helpless ladies living in packed conditions, and ethnic minorities might be unevenly impacted and have extra necessities. The utilization of mobile health and telemedicine to securely uphold those encountering savagery against women should be investigated desperately, just as different means to arrive at ladies in settings where admittance to cell phones or the web is restricted or lacking. Further, philanthropic associations need to make administrations accessible for ladies encountering brutality and gather information on detailed cases.

The reviewed literature gave an impression that domestic violence as a problem persists globally almost in all cultures irrespective of age, social class, status, education, and religion. It occurs in intimate relations within the household. It is understood that women of lower strata are more exposed to violence and in families that are more patriarchally organized. It is also found in the literature that upper and middle-class women are comparatively better in terms of education than lower-class women. Yet women of the upper, middle and lower class with education or without being exposed to some form of domestic violence. Moreover, poverty, marriage at an early year pushes women towards violence (Mishra, 2000). Gender socialization has relation with violence and the socialization process is responsible for domestic violence against women (Sahu, 2003).It is found that the husband and his relatives are involved in domestic violence but most of the studies reflected husbands' involvement in abusing their wives. Women of India are not only vulnerable to violence; women of china, Pakistan, Turkey, Ghana, America, the United Kingdom, etc. are equally facing the same because of a whole lot of issues discussed in the reviews. Studies showed that islamophobic dialogue sometimes conflicts with Muslim women which presents women as inactive and weak and makes them easily a victim of violence. Authoritarian family structure, breakdown of joint family system, drinking alcohol, suspicious and jealous attitude of husband, lack of mental preparedness for family, consumerist culture, lack of education, the financial status of the victims along with her family,etc. are some of the factors influencing domestic violence. These factors have a detrimental effect on women's social, economic, emotional, psychological, spiritual, reproductive, and sexual life. It increases the level of depression, anxiety, the suicidal tendency among women. Yet the women are not coming up with their problems. Muslim scholars viewed that Muslim women are emotionally abused yet they consider it as a dispute between husband and wife which is not a matter to be discussed in public. Women are being threatened to remarry because of the polygamy marriage system. Women find it difficult to show a denial of such behavior of husbands due to their financial dependence on husbands. The economic dependency of women on men is the main reason for which women do not leave their husbands or take any legal action against them. Aggressive behavior at home isn't the consequence of a solitary explanation rather it has been seen in literature that domestic violence is caused due to a mix of different other causes which has a serious impact on the reproductive and sexual health of women and affects women's life at various stages.

Women were suffering but hardly approached any support-providing agencies for seeking help. A study reflected that only 2% sought help that too when the women failed to compromise with the situation and the family environment became dangerous and threatening both for her and their children. Victims of sexual assault mostly approached medical services agencies and physical assault to legal services. It has also been reflected in the literature that most of the victims preferred to approach and sought help from informal agencies and the reason for such is financial exigencies. Lack of awareness about the available free legal aid services & medical care delivered through different formal organizations debarred women from availing timely support. In India, we have sufficient laws to protect women from any kind of violence but most of the time all the laws are failing when it comes to implementation. Victims are not properly heard by the support providing agencies and in some cases, agencies fail to get a proper response from the victim. It is found in the literature that women are not aware of socio-lawful help available for women under consideration. The writing mirrored that commitment of ladies in more prominent financial exercises in provincial regions might diminish the quantity of aggressive behavior at home; improved educational facilities would add to the decrease of abusive behavior at home against women; community-based education and awareness on socio-legal services ought to be made accessible including Self Help Groups, Non-Government Organisations, etc. for relooking at this issue. Victims should be provided with mobile health and telemedicine support services. Gender sensitization programs should be promoted in educational institutions. More and more research is expected on institutionalizing women's human rights; sexual instruction when marriage is important for couples. Literature stressed that victims need to be encouraged to register their complaints so that timely support can be extended to them. More or less advancement of monetary condition and education along with altered social patterns might protect women from this sort of brutality. There was a pressing need for a uniform civil code in works of literature. The literature suggested support providing agencies, government, non-government organizations, civil society may work in collaboration and cooperate to make the women more serene and violence-free.

The literature reflected the nature, causes, and impacts of abusive behavior at home alongside drives taken up by the support giving organizations and measures taken to end abusive behavior at home at national and international levels. The literature highlighted the legal services available for the women victims but the sources or the associations through which these services are given stayed uncovered. There were dearths of literature talking about the mechanisms through which services are provided to the women victims. The impact of domestic violence is broadly found in physical, sexual, and psychological aspects through these written works. However, there was less literature focusing impact on children, family life, and social life of the victim. Different factors of domestic violence were highlighted but the immediate reactions of the victim after violence have not been studied. Considering every one of these aspects, the current study has been designed to understand the perception of the victims about the violence and their immediate reaction to violence and the services provided by the support providing agencies along with its effectiveness in Cachar District of Assam.

Chapter - 3

Research Methodology

This chapter gives information regarding the methodology that has been adopted to conduct the study. It provides the details on the rationale of the study, research questions, objectives, samples, research design, sources of data, tools, data analysis.

3.1 Statement of the problem

Domestic violence is also known as gendered-based violence prevalent across the world. The government of India through different policies, programs, and Acts tried to combat issues related to domestic violence against women. The government introduced women police stations, rehabilitations schemes, shelter homes, family courts, helpline numbers etc. for distressed women.

Despite the means taken by the Government to forestall aggressive behavior against women at home, it keeps on being evil in our society. Women of the Northeastern region enjoy greater mobility in comparison to women of other communities of the country. However, Assam paints a contrasting picture in comparison to the other states of the North-East with regards to crime against women. In accordance with the NCRB record 2016, cruelty by husband and sexual assault against women is the top reported crime facing women in India.

As per NCRB information, 32.6% of cases were reported under the category of 'cruelty by a husband or his relatives and 25% cases reported under Assault on a woman, and 19% & 11.5% under kidnapping and abduction & rape respectively in 2016. NCRB also reveals that as per figure 2020, for the fourth times Assam has recorded the highest rate of crime against women. In 2017, the pace of wrongdoing against women in Assam was 143.3 followed by 166 in 2018 and 177 in 2019. In 2020, Assam recorded 26 examples of assault cum-murder/assault the third most elevated figure in the country after Uttar Pradesh (31) and Madhya Pradesh (27). It recorded 1,658 instances of assault a year ago. There were 4,642 instances of attack with the expectation of offending unobtrusiveness (Hindustan times, 19th April 2020).

The field survey in the Cachar district for the present study revealed that on an average 30-40 cases are reported monthly in the organizations dealing with domestic violence issues. According to chief functionaries of these organizations, the number of filing cases of domestic violence both by the Muslim and Hindu, Christian women's are increasing with the time which is crossing the rate of other crimes. Data reflects that domestic violence is assaulting thousands of women around the globe which needs to be addressed adequately. The available data highlighted the sorry plight of women in general where it is equally important to figure out religion-wise women victims of cruelty by husbands and other crimes in the study area. So realizing the depth of the issue present problem has been stated as Muslim Women and Domestic Violence: A Study in Cachar District.

3.2 Rationale of the study

The study has been led in the Cachar district of Assam contemplating the extending pace of crime against women. The District is located in the southernmost part of Assam and is the oldest among the districts of Assam. As per the reports of the National Crime Records Bureau of India (NCRB), Cachar has selected probably the biggest number of crime against women (1166 cases) in 2019 itself. 664 cases alone have been recorded of brutality by spouse or husband's family members. The survey further adds that this number is followed by 317 instances of hijacking and kidnapping of ladies during the year. Bandita Bora, a female activist of Assam's battles for the assurance of privileges connected with women and girl children once said that women and girl children in Assam and especially in Cachar are in upset waters because of the expansion in crime against women there. In understanding to Quran, women enjoy several rights in Islam.But in reality, women's privileges are getting abused not on account of the religion yet by individuals who are related to such brutality.

According to the reports of various developmental organisations, working for women's wellbeing and uprightness in Cachar saw that the referenced figures are only a hint of something larger as there are many cases that go unregistered because of social predicaments and issues of family honor. Data collected from the field study in Cachar district by the researcher revealed that Muslim gets the second most noteworthy situation after Hindu underlines the significance of concentrating on abusive behavior at home religion savvy to totally eradicate it from the society.

Hence, the study is an endeavor to comprehend the overall situation of domestic violence alongside various elements related to it against Muslim women in the Cachar district of

Assam. Support providing organizations available in Cachar like One-stop center, DLCCIW, SwadharGreh, family court, family counselingcenter are trying their best to resolve family conflicts and stretching out a wide range of help to victims of abusive behavior at home. Earlier these institutions had less acknowledgment by the general public however with the progression of time seeing the developmental activities of these institutions; society began approaching them with an assistance seeking behavior.

Alongside the individual voluntary social workers started taking a keen interest in the welfare of the society and became active in solving family issues. Hence, the study will make a detailed discussion on the effectiveness of these institutions in resolving the problems of the victim of domestic violence. Many literatures have covered studies conducted on the status of Muslim women in the Cachar district but a little research has been done on Domestic violence against Muslim women along with institutional services meant for curving such issue. The present study would venture in this direction. The findings of the study will be of immense help to all women, particularly Muslim women, educationists, department of social welfare, legal associates, police, health care providers, and, NGO professionals. Based on the findings needed policy can be formulated by the policymakers and approaches can be identified to combat the issue.

3.3 Objectives of the study

- To identify the casual factors leading to Domestic Violence among Muslim Women in Cachar district of Assam.
- To understand the effects of casual factors on the Muslim Women victims of Domestic Violence in Cachar District of Assam.
- To study the perceptions of the victims under consideration about the services provided by the support providing agencies in Cachar district of Assam.
- To identify the problems faced by the support providing agencies in delivering their services to the victims of Domestic Violence in Cachar District of Assam.

3.4 Research Questions

The present study focuses on the following research questions:

1. What are the nature and forms of domestic violence against Muslim women in Cachar district of Assam?
2. How do the factors of domestic violence affect a Muslim Women?
3. What is the perception of the victim of domestic violence about the efficacy of the services provided to them by the service providing agencies?

4. What support the victims are receiving from family members?
5. What is the procedure of providing services to the victims of domestic violence by the service providing agencies?
6. What are the problems faced by service providing agencies in delivering their services to victims of domestic violence?

3.5 The Universe of the Study

The area of the study was the Cachar District, Assam. All the Muslim women of the Cachar district constitute the universe of the study. There are many organisations of different status like Government & Non-Government does register the cases of domestic violence in the district.Among which a few are providing redressal services to the victims in a different manner. For the present study, initially, data on registered cases for the last five years, i.e. from 2014 to 2019, were collected from District Social Welfare, DLCCIW &SwadharGreh (Woodwichee, NGO) to determine the sample size. Among these organizations, DLCCIW and SwadharGreh under Woodwichee have been providing redressal services to the victims. Although the District Social Welfare, Cachar has been registering domestic violence cases, still they make a referred of these registered cases to the District Court for ensuring legal support and the Department of Social Welfare follows up on these cases. Among other organizations, the Family Court deals with the cases of family disputes and maintenance while the One-Stop Centre looks after cases related to domestic violence and provide unique services to vulnerable women for their upliftment.

Since the Centre has been in function since 2017, so in comparison to other organizations the number of registered cases is less but the unique features of the center have drawn the attention of the present study, especially considering the objective of studying the women victims' perception about the service providing agencies. The One Stop Centre, along with DLCCIW and SwadharGreh (Woodwichee) has been included in the study for determining the sample size. Therefore, the time frame of the study has been brought down to three years i.e. (January 2017 to 2019 December). The researcher collected data on registered cases of domestic violence for the last three years (i.e., 2017, 2018 & 2019) from the official records of the mentioned organizations and after further exclusion of the cases from the total number of registered cases based on religion and gender, only 128 cases found relevant for the present study. Thus the researcher has selected all the 128 respondents by adopting the census method for the study.

3.6 Research Design

The descriptive research design has been selected for the study to describe the situation of Muslim Women in India in general and Cachar District in specific from a broader perspective and to identify the causal factors responsible for occurring domestic violence.It also focuses on the effects of casual factors among the victims of domestic violence along with their perception about domestic violence and the services provided by the service providing agencies.

3.7 Methods and Tools of Data Collection

In this study, both qualitative and quantitative method was applied to gather data. Both primary and secondary sources were used to gather information. Primary sources included interaction with the victim, chief functionaries and officials of the select organisations through an interview schedule. The secondary sources of data were collected through consultation with previous research work, relevant books, journals, and publications, Government reports, mass media products, web information, websites, etc.

3.8 Data Analysis and Interpretation

The data collected were tabulated and analyzed with the help of Microsoft Excel software. The findings of the study are presented in the form of Tables, Diagrams, and Graphs.

3.9 Limitation of the Study

The limitations of the study are mentioned below:

1. The study is limited to only in Cachar district which restricts the study of other districts which could have presented a different picture.
2. The study was only limited to three organizations Like- DLCCIW, Sakhi One Stop Centre, and SwadharGreh (Woodwichee) where Domestic Violence cases were registered and did not include other organizations which were working for DV in the Cachar district.
3. The study only covered the registered cases of domestic violence against Muslim women in Cachar.

3.10 Operational Definition of the key terms

Violence: any act concerning physical power to hurt, injure and threaten to kill women.

Domestic Violence: an abusive behavior against women at home intends to assault women physically, mentally, sexually, and emotionally affecting women and children in family relationships.

Abuse: Treating women with cruelty and violence including physical, mental, emotional, and sexual.

Brutality: being cruel to wife.

Viciousness: aggressive and angry behaviour of husband towards wife at home.

3.11 Field Experience

Domestic violence is the topic of the time and is growing at a greater pace. During the pendency of the research work, the researcher had worked with the organizations addressing domestic violence issues in the Cachar District of Assam. The researcher has also interviewed with 128 women respondents, for having a first-hand understanding of the research problem. The researcher has also attempted to understand the challenges being faced by the members of the organization for having organizational shortcomings and also by gathering feedback from the victims of domestic violence concerning the areas where they feel they could have been helped in a better manner had there been more facilities (mainly in terms of securing livelihood).

Since the study area was Cachar and the scholar herself is an inhabitant of the said District, the researcher personally found it easier in terms of building good relationships with the respondents and the organizations working in the area. The researcher found both the organizations and respondents very much cooperative and therefore all sorts of the required information was possible to collect in time.

But the sudden outbreak of COVID-19 had affected the study for quite a long time. The researcher neither could physically visit the organizations nor the respondents who were interviewed during the data collection process. A situation came when the researcher had to go with telephonic interviews. But the researcher could not practice the same for long. Respondents were hesitant to speak over phone on an issue like domestic violence. The researcher waited for some time and when everything made opened the researcher conducted home visits to the victims.

It was indeed a challenge for the researcher to collect the required information from the victims of domestic violence. Since this is a very sensitive issue hence many a time it took a longer time than usual to collect data. In some cases, organisation working with the victim of domestic violence had to pitch in to make them feel confident enough to share information concerning them.

Besides, the researcher had to face a lot of difficulties in taking views of Muslim religious leaders on domestic violence. As they believe such cases of violence doesn't require any legal or formal procedure to settle cases. Such cases can be resolved as per the laws of

Shariat (Muslim Personal Laws). But, upon meeting with the victims of such cases whose grievance has been resolved by Islamic religious leaders, in many such cases the victim is found to be unsatisfied, those who had approached to the local Panchayat and local religious leaders seeking solution of their problems. As a result there are many cases when the victim and her family had approached police and civil court for justice.

The researcher's experience of meeting and understanding the Islamic religious leaders and their informal laws/ norms to resolve issues about domestic violence are very much inclined towards patriarchal culture. Hence, most of the women who were interviewed expressed dissatisfaction with the problem-solving procedures and decision-making process either by the Panchayat or local religious leaders. The researcher has also observed that in most of the cases those involved in conflict resolution are predominantly male. Women as such have been barred from becoming a member of the unit of conflict resolvers. And, as a result, it leads to a state of helplessness too for the victim in some cases.

During the process of data collection, the researcher has interviewed victims of domestic violence who are still facing violence despite their cases being resolved informally at the Panchayat level by the informal leaders as per community norms. But, violence continued as revealed by the victim during the process of the interview. The victim further stated that due to extreme poverty her family members are not in a position to fight legal battles. As a result, out of no alternative, she is suffering.

No doubt service-providing agencies have played an active role to assist the victims of domestic violence with awareness, legal aid, and resources. However, upon taking feedback from the victims of domestic violence, they feel there are a lot of areas where the organization could work to improve upon the conditions of the victims of domestic violence. Firstly, the setup or informal committee which is working at the village level must have enough learned women representatives to make sure every case finds its just conclusion. Secondly, the organization must work towards assisting the divorced or separated women to lead a self-sufficient life economically by helping them attain some or other livelihood skills. Thirdly, victims of such violence who are not economically good enough to fight legal battles must be identified through regular visits and helped to fight their case. Fourthly, a case must be dealt with in totally that is a victim must be helped enough to start her life being a wife, a divorcee, or a separated woman. The victim shall not be left by any particular agency once they feel they have done enough for the victim rather they should try to connect the victim with the needed organization, so to make sure, they are not left helpless.

Lastly, the researcher feels as if the structure of our society is male-dominated, so a woman takes years to reveal the violence they had suffered. In this regard, the researcher thinks local and international NGOs, intellectuals, and government organizations must work together to make the environment good enough so that women could come out and seek justice easily.

Chapter - 4

Study Area: Cachar District, Assam

The current study has been led in the district of Cachar, Assam. Assam is the largest state as far as population is concerned and stands second with regards to Geographical area among the eight North-Eastern regions. The state is surrounded by different other states. In North, the state has Arunachal Pradesh and Bhutan; in East, it has Manipur, Nagaland; in West, Meghalaya, Bangladesh & West Bengal and in South, the state has Mizoram and Tripura. Assam has two distinctive regions like Brahmaputra Valley and Barak Valley. The Barak Valley consists of three districts and the valley Brahmaputra has 32 districts. Altogether Assam has 35 districts.

Map of Assam containing all districts

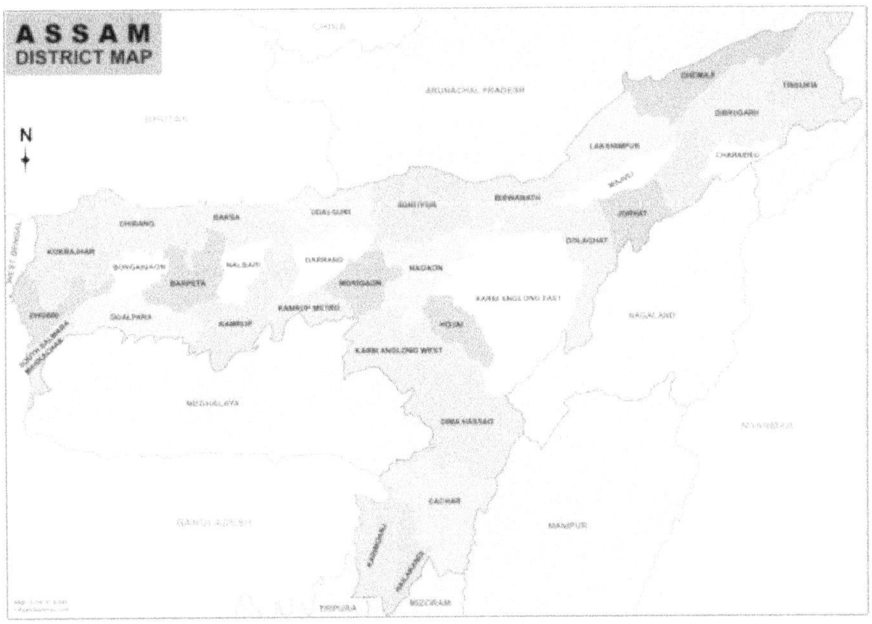

Diagram 4.1: Map of Assam containing all districts

4.1 The Barak Valley

The southern part of Assam is dedicated to Barak Valley with Cachar, Karimganj&Hailakandi as its districts. The absolute populace of Barak Valley according to the census of 2011 is 3,624,599.

Cachar has 5 circles namely Sonai, Katigorah, Silchar, Udharbond&Lakhipur. Karimganj also has 5 circles named Badarpur, Karimganj, Nilam bazaar, Patharkandi, Ramkrishna Nagar, and the district Hailakandi has four circles Algapur, Hailakandi, Katlichera, Lala.

Map of Barak Valley containing three districts Cachar (Silchar), Hailakandi and Karimganj

Diagram 4.2: Map of Barak Valley containing three districts Cachar (Silchar), Hailakandi and Karimganj

4.2 District Wise population

Table 4.1: District Wise population

Sl. No	District	Population	
		Hindu	Muslim
1.	Cachar	1038985	654816
2.	Hailakandi	251194	397653
3.	Karimganj	521962	629489

Source: Census 2011

The 2011 census reflects that Silchar, Lakhipur, and Udharbond are among the five circles of Cachar district having a Hindu majority population, and Sonai, Katigorah circle is with the Muslim majority population. Katlichera and Lalacirlcle of Hailakandiensures Hindu majority when in Algapur and Hailakandi, Muslims are majority. In Karimganj two circles named Ramkrishna Nagar and Patharkandi are with Hindu larger part and in KarimganjNilambazar, Badarpur circles are high with Muslim populace according to census 2011.

4.3 Cachar District-At a Glance

4.3.1 Area and Location

The district Cachar is the oldest among the districts of Assam. It was made after the extension of the Kachari realm by the British in 1830. Later, North Cachar was added and labeled to the area in 1854. Further, North Cachar Sub-Division was made into a different area and removed from Cachar in 1951. Subsequently, the Karimganj subdivision and Hailakndi subdivision was made a different district in 1983 and 1989 respectively. The district is situated in the southernmost part of the state. It is encircled by Barail and Jayantia Hills in the north; the state Mizoram is in the south and Manipur in the east; Karimganj&Hailakandi is in the west. The district has an international border with Bangladesh.

4.3.2 Administrative Division

Cachar has an area of 3,786 sq. Km., with two sub-divisions named Silchar and Lakhipur. The headquarter of the district is Silchar. It has 163 no.GaonPanchayats, 15 no.AnchalikPanchayats, 1 no.ZillaParishad, 15 no.Development Blocks, 7 no.Townsand 5 no.Revenue Circles.

Map of Cachar districts

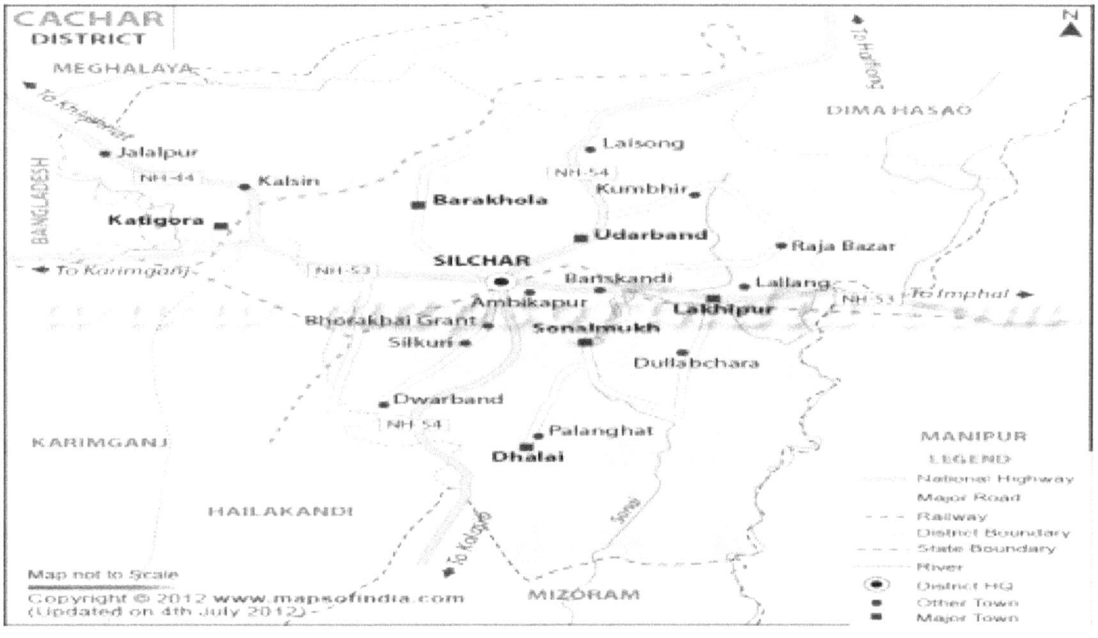

Diagram 4.3: Map of Cachar District

4.4 Resource Base of the District

4.4.1 Population of the District

The population of Cachar is 1,736,617 as per census of 2011. Among which 8, 86,284 are male and 8, 50,333 female. The census data indicates that 86.06 percent of the total population belongs to rural areas.

Table 4.2: Total Population of Cachar district

Description	Total Population	Rural	Urban
Total Population	1,736,617	14,21,153	3,15,464
Male Population	8,86,284	7,27,083	1,59,201
Female Population	8,50,333	6,94,070	1,56,263

Source: Census of India 2011

Table 4.3: Religion wise distribution of population in Cachar District

Sl. No.	Religion	Percentage of population
1.	Hindu	59.83%
2.	Muslim	37.71%
3.	Christians	2.17%
4.	Sikhs	0.02%
5.	Buddhists	0.02%
6.	Jains	0.10%
7.	Others	0.01%

Source: Census of India, 2011

4.5 Gender ratio of the District

The best way to understand gender equality is the study of sex ratio i.e. quantity of females per thousand males. Cachar district has a sex proportion of 958 females for every 1000 males (District Profile, Govt. of Assam). It has 256774 children aged 0-6 years, of which, 131417 male and 125357 female kids. According to the census 2011, the sex ratio of a child in the Cachar district is 954 which is lower than the average sex ratio of Cachar district i.e. 959. The sex ratio based on caste and religion mirrors that the Hindus and the SC populace have a low sex proportion in contrast with Muslims in the area (Cachar District Population, Caste, Religion Data (Assam) - Census 2011.

4.6 Educational status of the District

The district's average literacy rate stands at 79.34 percent. Male literates are 84.78% while 73.68 percent of females are literate in the district. The rural areas of Cachar district have a 78.14 percent literacy rate and 89.77 percent in urban areas. The rural and urban male literacy rates are 84.27 percent and 92.69 percent respectively whereas for rural females it is 71.71 percent and for urban females, it is 86.8 percent. An analysis of these figures indicates that although the female literacy rate shows an upward trend it remains lower than male literacy. The female literacy rate of 2001 was 59.41 percent which reached to 74.62 percent in 2011.

The above figures reflect that in comparison to female literacy, male literacy is higher. However, expanded development of education rate among country ladies has been noticed. According to the 2001 census, the education rate of females was 55.94 percent and it rose to 71.71 percent in 2011. However, urban women share different literacy figures. Largely, the literacy rate of rural women is much lesser than urban women. From this, it tends to be induced that women of Cachar district have always been in the second situation in contrast with their male partners. By and large, the lower literacy rate of females is considered as the basic cause of domestic violence against women in the Cachar district.

Table 4.4: Literacy Rates by Sex in Cachar District: 2001 and 2011 (In per cent)

Literacy Rate	Area	2001			2011		
		Person	**Male**	**Female**	**Person**	**Male**	**Female**
	Total	67.82	75.73	59.41	80.36	85.85	74.62
	Rural	65.25	74	55.94	78.14	84.27	71.71
	Urban	86.76	91.09	82.23	89.77	92.69	86.8

Source: Census of India, 2001 & 2011

Religion savvy education rate uncovers that the proficiency pace of Hindus is higher in urban and Muslim's proficiency rate is higher in rural areas. However, the female education pace of

Hindus and Muslims is practically something very similar in rural areas. But overall literacy rate of Muslim females is lower than that of Hindus. In contrast, Muslim male education is better than that of Hindus.

Table 4.5: Religion wise literacy rate with place of residence in Cachar (in percentage)

Religion	Residence	Person	Male	Female
Hindus	District Total	79.34	84.78	73.68
Hindus	Rural	77.08	83.12	70.75
Muslims	District Total	88.99	91.59	85.99
Muslims	Rural	77.08	83.12	70.75

Source: Census of India, 2011

4.7 Work force of Cachar District: Total, Main, Marginal & Non Workers

Whereas in 2011 census data out of total workers (6, 08,062) the main workers are (5, 71,259) and for marginal workers, it is (1, 36,803). If we look at the male-female distribution of both main and marginal workers we shall see that the male main workers (3, 95,681) are higher than male marginal workers (74,071). But it is interesting to note that in the Cachar district among the total female workers (1, 38,310), the main female workers (75,578) are lower than the marginal workers (62,732). The number of female non workers (7, 12,023) is higher than male non workers (4, 16,532). This implies that women prefer to go for part-time work as it will enable them to devote full attention to household responsibilities as well. As a result of this, they become financially dependent on male members of families. It can thus be inferred that a large segment of the women population remains non-workers in terms of economic activities; and that they are dependent on men for sustenance.

Table 4.6: Distribution of Main Workers, Marginal Workers and Non Workers in Cachar District

Person/ Male/ Female	Total Workers	Main Workers	Marginal Workers	Non Workers
Person	6,08,062	5,71,259	1,36,803	11,28,555
Male	4,69,752	3,95,681	74,071	4,16,532
Female	1,38,310	75,578	62,732	7,12,023

Source: Census of India 2011

4.7.1 Participation of Female in Work

Female participation in work helps us to understand the rate and nature of women's engagement in economic activities and also their economic self-reliance. The below table presents the work rate participation of females in the Cachar district.

Table 4.7: Female Work Participation Rate in Cachar District (In percent)

Year	Work Participation Rate
2001	13.6
2011	14.43

Source: Census of India 2001 & 2011

The female work participation rate was 13.6 percent as per the 2001 census and 14.43 percent in 2011. The statistics indicated a nominal increase in work participation of females i.e. from 13.6 to 14.43 percent but it remained less than 20 percent. It is assumed from the figures that the participation of women in work is poor in the district. A lower rate of work participation indicates women's dependence on their male partners and as per literature economic dependence is one of the important factors of domestic violence against women.

4.8 Organisation working on Domestic Violence in Cachar

Cachar has both Government and Non-Government Organisations addressing the issue of domestic violence. These organizations are working either independently or in collaboration. District Court, District legal services authority, family court, department of social welfare, etc are a few of the Government organizations dealing with domestic violence issues. In most of the cases district, social welfare makes a referral the cases to the district court and follows up. Family court deals with maintenance-related matters of victims of domestic violence. Alongside organizations like one-stop center has been created by the Government with shelter home facility for the victims. District level committee for a crime involving women, SwadharGreh, Woodwichee is a voluntary organization extending support to women facing aggressive behavior at home in different forms in the district. Their unique services made scope in the study for making discussion on them. Thus, these three organizations have been selected to get the respondents who registered their cases in either of the organizations and sought support. A brief about the organizations is discussed below.

District Level Committee for Crime Involving Women (DLCCIW), Silchar: Cachar

District Level Committee for Crime Involving Women was set up by the Deputy Commissioner, Cachar, Assam vide office notice No.CCL.25/9742, dated-20/05/1997 to resolve different issues faced by the women. The main purpose of the Committee is to take all possible steps to eradicate various types of crimes being committed against a woman which has been increasing at a menacing rate in the District of Cachar, Assam. In many cases, due to illiteracy and poverty, the womenfolk are not in a position to get proper justice from the existing system. Quite often they are also not aware of the legal safeguards available to them and they do not get proper guidance at night time. The Committee's office is often for the public on all days from 10 AM. To 4 PM, except on Govt. holidays. Besides the main Committee, the Thana level committee is also taking up cases when people approach them. Another eight committees, attached to eight police stations in the Cachar district being named "Police Station Level Committee for Crimes Involving Women" were also set up of which the parent committee is "The District Level Committee for Crime Involving Women" with the same view & purpose. The Police Station Level Committee acts as the model agency at the police station level.

Sakhi One Stop Centre

The center started functioning in 2017 in the Cachar district of Assam with a plan to offer coordinated help and support to women impacted by savagery under one rooftop. The center has also planned to facilitate women, and victims, with crisis and non-crisis support services immediately which includes clinical, lawful, mental, counseling & guidance to battle against any types of viciousness against women. The OSC support all ladies including young ladies under 18 years old impacted by savagery, regardless of caste, class, religion, area, sexual direction, or conjugal status. For young ladies under 18 years old, foundations and specialists are laid out under the Juvenile Justice (Care and Protection of Children) Act, 2000.

SwadharGreh (Woodwichee)

Perceiving the requirement for momentary asylum, the SwadharGreh Scheme is run by the Ministry of Women and Child Development to give accommodation temporarily, maintenance, and rehabilitative services to homeless women and girls. In the district, Wodwichee (NGO) has been running the SwadharGreh scheme since 2005. SwadharGreh is accommodating women for maximum period of 5 years. An elderly woman above 55 years may be kept in the Swadhar till he/she attains the age of 60. After that the concerned elderly will be shifted to old age homes. SwadharGreh is not open for women of mental disabilities rather they are shifted to a mental rehabilitation center to appropriately guarantee that their requirements are met. The facilities offered by the SwadharGreh are also enjoyed by the children accompanying women. Young ladies up to the age of 18 years and young boy up to the age of 12 years is permitted to remain in the SwadharGreh with their mothers and the boy above 12 years of age is shifted to the Children Homes run under JJ Act/ICPS).

Table 4.8: A Glimpse of the registered cases of Domestic Violence in precedent years

Year	**Name of the organisation**	**Total Registered cases of DV**	**Cases Registered under Muslim Religion**	**Cases Registered by Muslim Women**
2014-2019	DLCCIW	626	123	91
2014-2019	SwadharGreh (Woodwichee)	87	49	49
2017-2019	Sakhi One Stop Centre	95	44	44
Total		808	216	184

Although women in India are worshipped as goddesses, they nonetheless confront a variety of women's issues such as domestic abuse, rape, dowry, and harassment. Regardless of significant advancement of women in different fields, and a historic evidence of women advocacy, viciousness against women keeps on being a warned theme. As previously noted, cases are still being recorded, and the severity of the situation, as well as the ongoing intake of cases, warrants an investigation into the scope of the problem in Barak Valley and its consequences. The findings are summarised in Chapter 5, which covers each of the study's objectives.

Presentation & Discussions of Findings

The present chapter provides information about the findings of the study conducted on Muslim Women and Domestic Violence in the Cachar District of Assam. Information has been collected on different variables. Therefore, it has helped the researcher to analyze and interpret the responses accordingly. The first objective of the study was to identify the causal factors leading to Domestic Violence among Muslim Women in the Cachar district of Assam. The interview schedule for the said objective has been divided into four sections i) Demographics and socio-economic profile; ii) Nature and extent of domestic violence; iii) Factors leading to domestic violence; iv) Types of domestic violence faced by the respondents. The second objective of the study was to understand the effects of causal factors on Muslim Women victims of Domestic Violence in Cachar District of Assam. For which the interview schedule contained sections like i) Effects of causal factors; ii) Compelling factors for continuing with the abusive relationship; iii) Help-seeking approach of the respondents; iv) Help received by the respondents; v) Nature of reporting cases. The third objective was to study the Perceptions of the victims under consideration about the services provided by the support-providing agencies in the Cachar District of Assam. Thus, the interview schedule has been formulated with the sections like i) Awareness about support providing agencies along with their services; ii) Type of services received by the respondents; iii) Perception of the respondents about the services provided; iv) Factors of satisfaction; v) Measures suggested for improving the quality of services and reducing domestic violence issues. The last objective of the study was to understand the problems faced by the support providing agencies in delivering their services to the victims of Domestic Violence in the Cachar District of Assam. Therefore, the interview schedule has been designed with such sections which help to get accurate information on the set objective. The sections were i) Profile of the organization; ii) Functions of the organization; iii) Nature of cases registered; iv) Process of dealing with the cases; v) Problems faced in delivering services; vi) Approaches adopted in response to the problem' vii) Suggestions for improving the service delivery. The responses have been collected under each head and presented through diagrams, figure and tables.

5.1 Demographic and Socio-Economic Profile

5.1.1 Age of the Respondent

It is found in the literature that young women are at high risk of aggressive behavior at home in contrast with women of the elder age group. The survey on National Family Violence conducted in America demonstrated that most women below 30 years of age face all forms of domestic violence. The present study will analyze this contention and will evaluate the degree of such a contention in the instances of respondents covered by the study. The below figure shows the age-wise classification of the respondents selected for the study. They were grouped into six age groups: 18-22 years, 23-27 years, 28-32 years, 33-37 years, 38-42 years, and above 42 years of age. The figure below depicts the respondents' age groups:

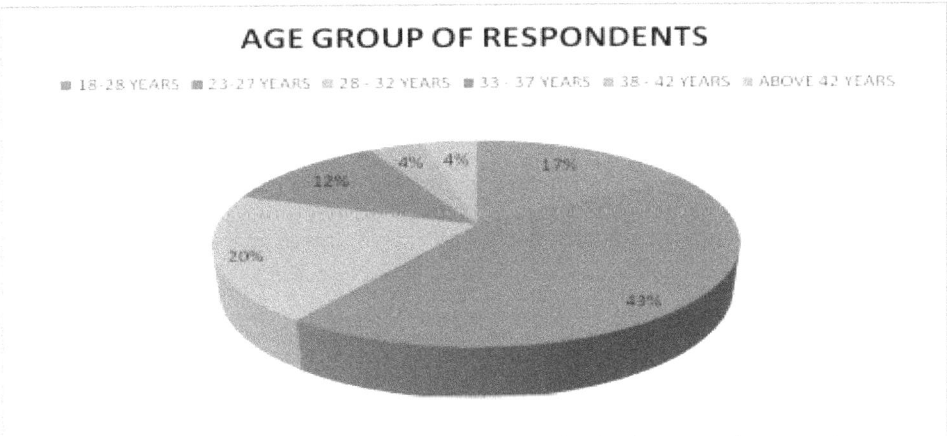

Figure 5.1: Age group of the respondents

Figure 5.1, presented above shows that about 43% of the respondents are in the age group of 23-27 years, followed by 20% from the ages of 28-32 years & 17 percent of the respondents are in the ages of 18-22 years. Around 12% of the respondents are from 33-37 years and about 4% are between the ages of 38-42 and above 42 years respectively. It emphasizes that, even though the majority of the victims are between the ages of 23 and 27, violence is perpetrated against people of all ages, including late adults.

5.1.2 Age of Marriage

Age of marriage is a significant variable in the investigation of domestic violence against women. The early age of marriage may create ample scope of stress for both couples. It can thus be assumed those women getting married at an early age are at higher risk of being mishandled by their spouses or potentially parents-in-law. The information relating to the age at marriage of the respondents has been collected to understand the connection between the degree of viciousness and the age at marriage. The following table shows respondents' age of marriage and their present age.

Table 5.1: Age of Marriage and Present Age

Current	**Age of Marriage**			
Age group	16-20	21-25	26-30	Total
18-22	19 (14.84%)	3 (2.34%)	0	22 (17.18%)
23-27	31 (24.22%)	20 (15.63%)	4 (3.12%)	55 (42.97%)
28-32 10 (7.81%)		14 (10.94%)	2 (1.65%)	26 (20.31%)
33-37	8 (6.25%)	5 (3.91%)	2 (1.56%)	15 (11.72%)
38-42	3 (2.344%)	1 (0.78%)	1 (0.78%)	5 (3.91%)
Above 42	3 (2.3444%)	1 (0.78%)	1 (0.78%)	5 (3.91%)
Total	74 (57.81%)	44 (34.38%)	10 (7.81%)	128 (100%)

The above data connecting with the age of respondents at marriage presented in table 5.1 shows that the majority of the respondents (42.97 percent) are between the ages of 23-27. Among which 24.22 percent married at the age of 16-20 years. 15.63 married at 21-25 and just 3.12 percent married at 26-30 years.

The next age group to report abuse is those between the ages of 28-32, which accounts for 20.31 percent of all respondents. Among which 7.81 percent married between 16-20 years of age, 10.94 percent at 21-25 age; 1.65 percent at the age of 26-30 years.

17.19 percent of the respondents who reported abuse are from the ages of 18-22. Among them, 14.84 percent married at the age of 16-20 years; 2.34 percent at 21-25. No information was reported under the 26-30 age groups.

About 11.72 percent of the respondents who reported abuses are from the age group of 33-37. Among them 6.25 percent of respondents married at the age of 16-20 years; 3.91 percent between the ages of 21-25 and 1.56 percent from the age group of 26-30.

The lowest category constitutes 3.91 percent of respondents belong to the ages of 38-42 and 42 above. Among the respondents, 3.444 percent married at 16-20 years; 0.78 percent at 21-25 and 0.78 percent between the ages of 26-30 respectively.

It adds that the majority of Muslim victims married when they were 16-20 years old (57.81 percent) and immediately faced domestic violence, with the majority (42.97 percent) disclosing their abuse by the time they were 23-27 years old.

5.1.3 Nature of marriage of the Respondents

Marriage is a union of two people in a personal relationship. It is a primary institution that brings common goodness to society by building families and procreating children. It is generally expected that the Marriage will take place with the consent of family members even in case of mutual likings of the boy and girl. Literature captured that the women who have undergone arranged marriages are more prone to domestic violence perpetrated by their husbands and family members. This background knowledge influenced the researcher to understand the type of marriage followed by the respondents and its relation with domestic violence (figure 5.2).

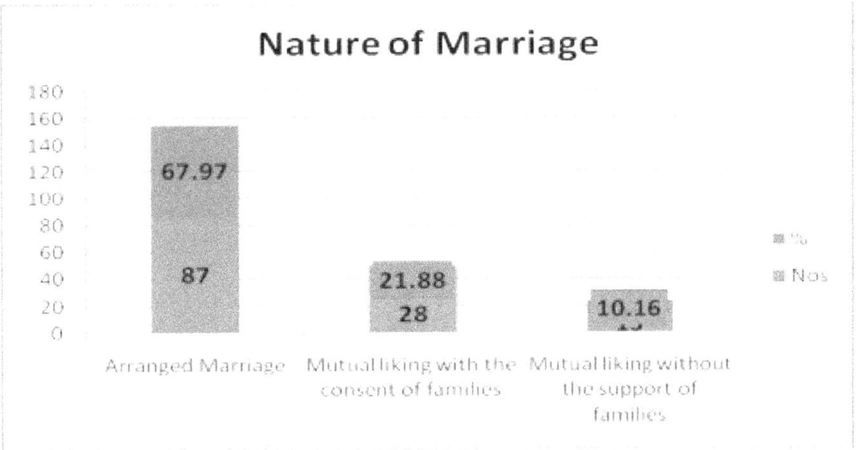

Figure 5.2: Nature of marriage of the respondents

The above data presented through figure 5.2, reflects that the majority of the respondents i.e. 67.97 percent had arranged marriage with the consent of family members. 21.88 percent of the respondents married the person whom they liked with the consent of family members. 10.16 percent of the respondents had mutual likings but they had to marry without the support of family members. According to the findings, the majority of Muslim marriages that result in domestic violence are arranged by family members. Thus, women begin their lives with strangers, are abused, and eventually divorce.

5.1.4 Marital Status of the respondents

It is by and large expected that abusive behavior at home is an exceptional peculiarity wherein just wedded ladies are involved. But truly any woman either married, unmarried, separated, divorced or widow is the victim of abusive behavior at home perpetrated by people on whom the woman is reliant. There are some situations where women remain unmarried and thus stay with their parents and brothers. In such cases, many a time the woman faces torture by her siblings and spouses. Thus to gather information in this regard the researcher collected data about the marital status of the respondents. The findings are presented through the underneath (figure 5.3).

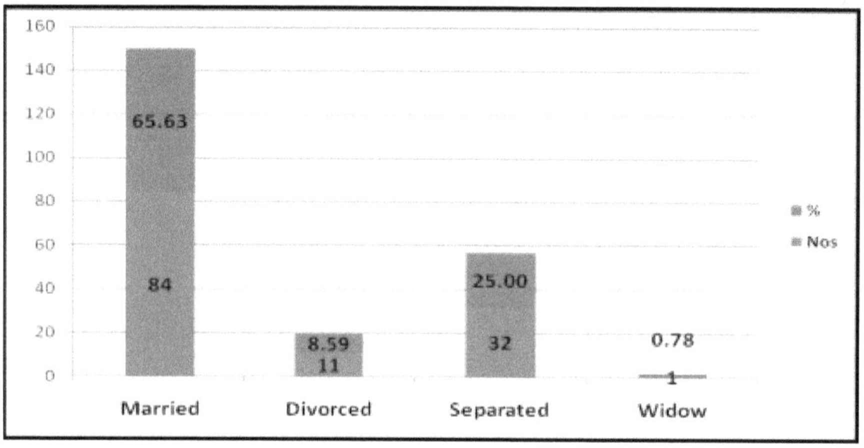

Figure 5.3: Marital Status of the respondents

Figure 5.3 relating to the marital status of the respondent's shows that 65.63 percent of respondents were reported as married. About 25 percent of the respondents were living separately from their husbands and were battling for divorce. About 8.59 percent of the respondents have already taken divorce and 0.78% of the respondents were reported as widows.

5.1.5 Type of Family

The family structure is a significant variable for comprehending the peculiarity of domestic violence against women. It is expected from the women to make adjustments with all the family members, be it joint, extended, or nuclear families. But in comparison to women of nuclear families, joint and extended families women are in a vulnerable situation. The patriarchal and authoritarian family structure put women of all religions in subservient positions. Men are likely to act like a son rather than a spouse. Parents in law keep on having a more prominent connection with their son than daughter in law which increases the possibility of viciousness against wives at home. Thus, it is assumed that a larger number of family members not just make the issue of change but sometimes they act as troublemakers for aggressive behavior at home against women.

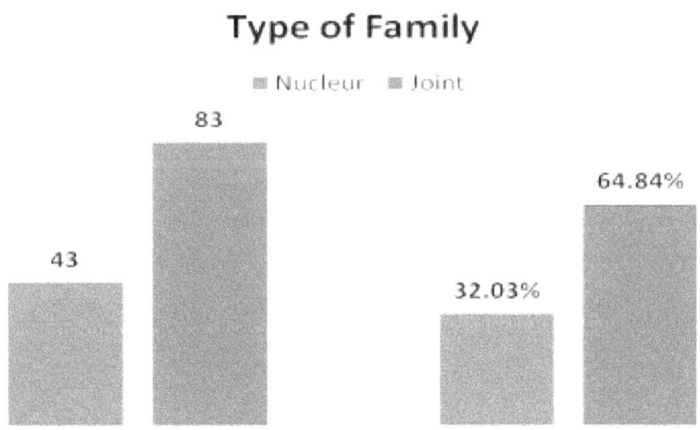

Figure 5.4: Type of Families to which respondents belong

Figure 5.4 related to the type of family indicated that out of 128 respondents covered by the study about 64.84 percent were living with joint families and 32.03 percent were from nuclear families. The data reflected that the majority of the domestic violence cases reported was from joint families.

5.2 Respondents' status with off-springs (children)

Children are said to be the soul of the family. They have the same human rights as adults and specific rights addressing their special needs. It is the right of the child to be provided with a conducive environment that leads their development to the fullest. But different circumstances put children in a difficult situation and domestic violence is one such issue that affects children from all corners. At times having no children in a couple of relationships also leads to violence at home. Thus, the information about children's status has been collected to understand the parental status and the consequences the children may confront if they are exposed to domestic violence.

5.2.1 Respondents with off-springs

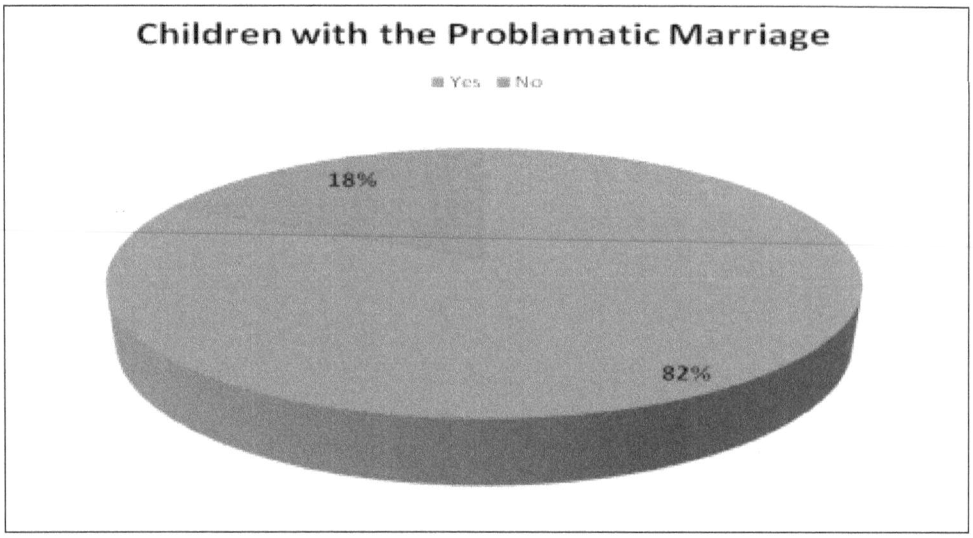

Figure 5.5: Respondents with off-springs

The data presented in above figure 5.5, shows that 82 percent of the respondents had children from the marriage in which the victims experienced maltreatment, whereas 18 percent had no children. As a result, a large number of respondents had to make a solid decision with regards to their and their kids' life so that a safe and secured life can be ensured. Respondents without children could start a new life without being reliant on others.

5.2.2 Educational Standard of the Respondents

Education has a significant role to play in human lives. Higher the degree of education, higher the capacity for opposing any activity of foul plays, abuse, and torture. Education gives women the confidence to raise their voices against the injustices that take place on them and empower them to battle for equality. Through formal education, women are made aware of different things happening in the environment which gives a scope to the women to understand life from a realistic point of view. Thus education extends the skyline and makes women more educated. Moreover, education supports women in ensuring economic sustainability and enhancing social status. In the study, the educational level of the respondents was studied to understand the relationship between the degree of education of women and the nature of the interpersonal relationship in context to domestic violence women.

The following figure 5.6 presents the information about the educational status of the respondents. The educational standard has been categorized into six parts illiterate, primary, middle school, HSLC, HS, graduate, Postgraduate.

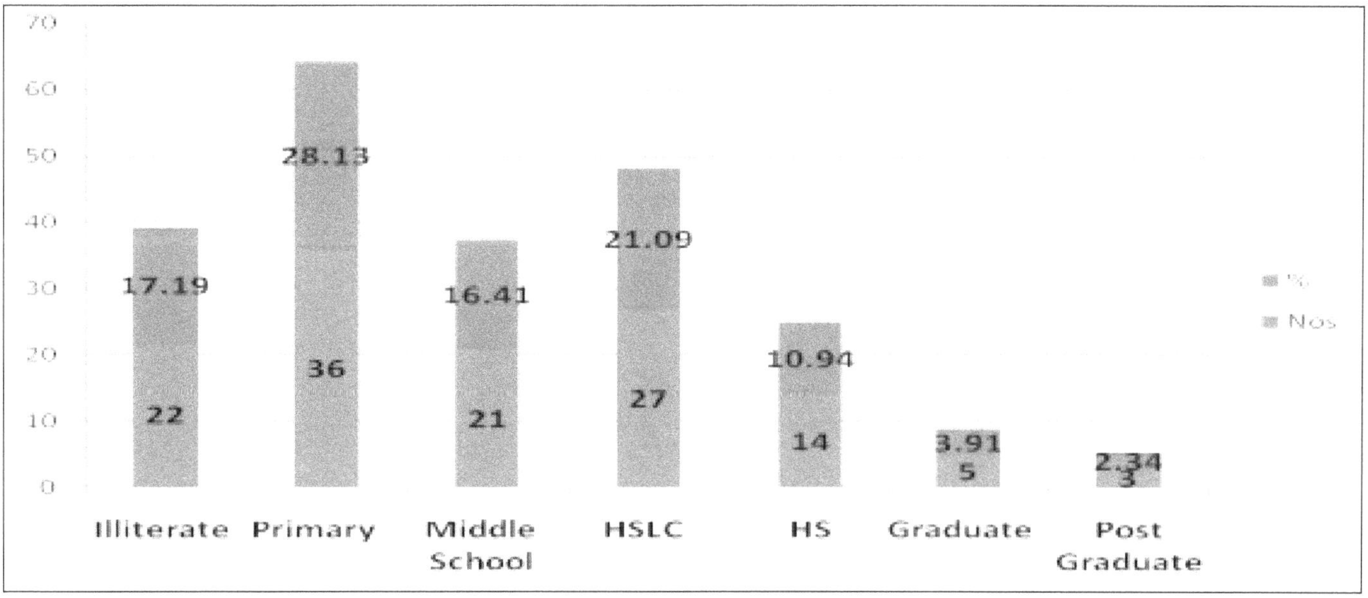

Figure 5.6: Educational Standard of the respondents

The statistical data presented in figure 5.6 shows that the majority of the respondents i.e. 28.13 percent had just primary school level or up to middle school (16.41 percent) level education. About 21.09 percent had education up to HSLC level and 10.94 educated up to HS level. Further, 3.91 percent of the respondents had graduated and only 2.34 percent had post-graduation. In addition, 17.19 percent of the respondents were illiterate. This explains the most of the Muslim women victims only had primary education.

5.2.3 Occupational background and Monthly Income of the respondents

The social status of women to a great extent is determined by their occupation. Good occupation gives women higher distinction in their families and the general public. Different studies demonstrated that women with lower levels of occupations are mishandled. Moreover, it is perceived that women who are at home and not occupied with paid work outside their homes are more at risk of being abused in comparison to women occupied with paid work outside their homes. With this background understanding the study intended to examine the relationship between the existence or nonexistence of occupation and the degree of domestic violence and also to learn more about the economic independence of battered women. Thus, the information related to the occupational background with monthly income has been collected and presented in table 5.2.

Table 5.2: Occupation and Monthly Income of the respondents

Occupational Background of the Respondents	Personal Monthly Income				
	No income	Less than Rs. 3000	Rs 3001- Rs. 6000	Above Rs 6000	TOTAL
Home maker	95 (74.22%)	0 (0.00)	0 (0.00)	0 (0.00)	95 (74.22%)
Job in Govt. & Pvt. Sector	0 (0.00)	8 (6.25%)	3 (2.34%)	1 (0.78%)	12 (9.38%)
Wage labour	0 (0.00)	0 (0.00)	0 (0.00)	1 (0.78%)	1 (0.78%)
House maid	0 (0.00)	7 (5.47%)	8 (6.25%)	2 (1.56%)	17 (13.28%)
Business Women	0 (0.00)	1 (0.78%)	0 (0.00)	2 (1.56%)	3 (2.34%)
TOTAL	95 (74.22%)	16 (12.50%)	11 (8.59%)	6 (4.69%)	128 (100%)

It can be viewed from the data presented in the above table that 74.22 percent of the respondents are homemakers with no income and thus no economic freedom. 13.28 percent of the respondents work as housemaids. Among them, 5.47 percent of respondents earned less than Rs. 3000/-; 6.25 percent earning between Rs. 3001-Rs. 6000 and 1.56 percent respondents earning more than Rs. 6000/-. About 9.38 percent of the respondents are working as fourth-grade employees in the private offices of the district. Among which 6.25 percent earning is less than Rs. 3000/-; 2.34 percent was earning between Rs. 3001-Rs. 6000/- and only 0.78 percent of the respondents earning was more than Rs. 6000/-. Only 2.34 percent of the respondents were looking after their own business. Among them 0.78 percent earning was less than Rs. 3000 and 1.56 percent had earned more than Rs. 6000/-.

Thus, more than half of the respondents were found to be homemakers followed by housemaids. The majority of them had no income and 12.50 percent had income less than Rs. 3000/- and only 4.69 percent had earn above Rs. 6000/-.

5.3 Nature and Extent of Domestic Violence

5.3.1 Perception about the nature of domestic violence

The perception of the respondents who were victims of domestic violence and had to suffer may differ from those who have not experienced any violence in their life. The perception about the issue depends upon the situation in which the victims find themselves and the availability of options to cope with the situation. The individuals who are manhandled within the sight of others are bound to feel embarrassed as they may foster a sensation of having been let down according to other people. To comprehend the perception of domestic violence, the respondents were asked to share their opinion about the nature of domestic violence. The responses were recorded through a multiple choice question and findings are presented through the following figure 5.7.

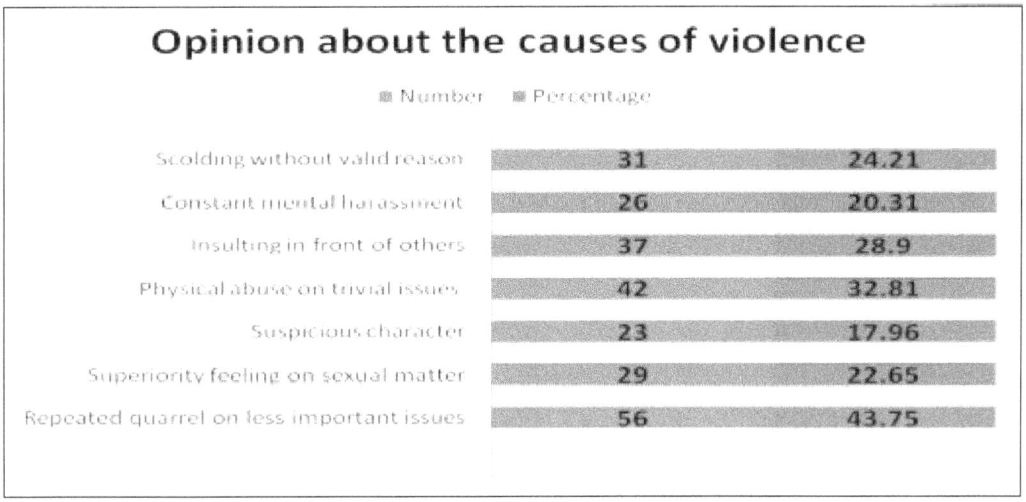

Figure 5.7: Nature and Extent of Domestic Violence

The reasons for the violence are explained in figure 5.7. About 24.21 percent of the respondents expressed that receiving scolding without any valid reason leads to violence. 20.31 percent of the respondents viewed that constant mental harassment leads to domestic violence and 28.90 percent opined that the attitude of insulting in front of others my husband and family members causes invite domestic violence. Around 17.96 percent of the respondents stated that the suspicious character of the husband invites conflicting situations at home and 22.65 percent of respondents viewed that the dominant feeling of husbands in sexual matters is a cause of domestic violence. About 32.81 percent of the respondents thought that physical abuse on trivial issues often leads to violence at home. According to 43.75 percent of the respondents, domestic violence happens because of repeated quarrels on less important issues.

5.3.2 Instigators of Domestic Violence

Instigation is very much associated with domestic violence. It is noticed that someone among the family members acts as a trouble maker of violence. Such individuals might be spouses, relatives, in-laws, etc. The respondents were asked to share about the instigators who instigated the violence against them. The responses have been recorded through multiple choice questions and presented in figure 5.8. There were numerous instigators in the majority of instances, and in rare cases, it was just the husband.

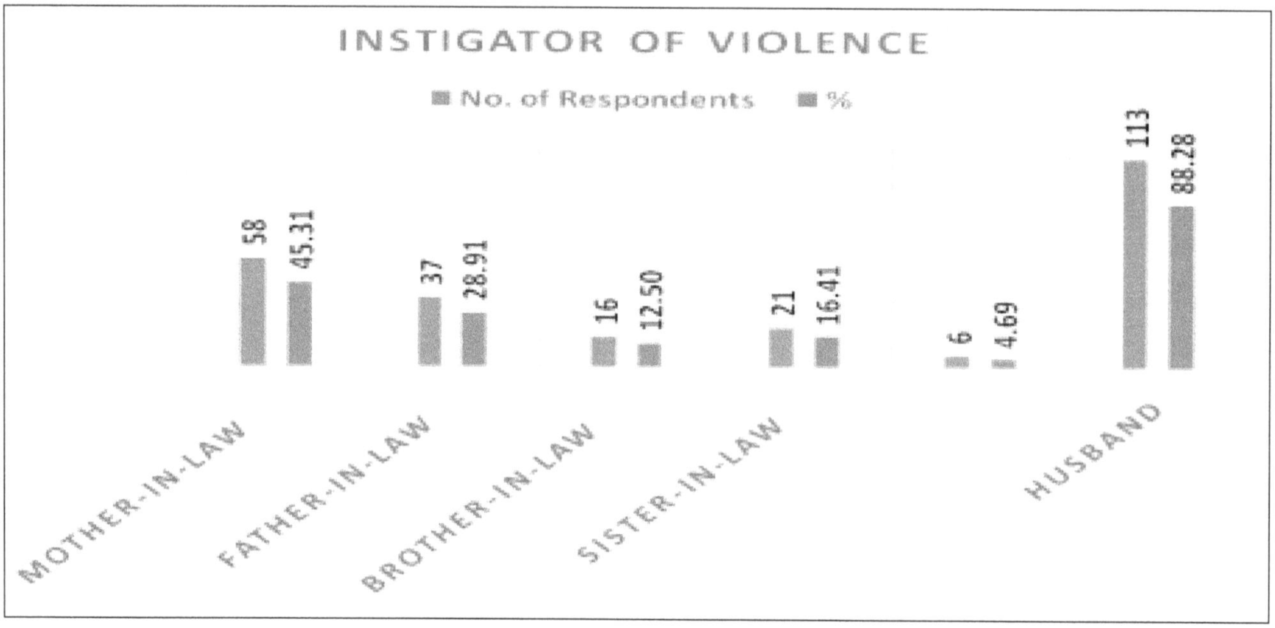

Figure 5.8: Instigators of domestic Violence

The data presented in the above figure 5.8 indicates that the husband was the frequent instigator of domestic violence as reported by 88.28 percent of the total respondents. 45.31 percent of the respondents accused mother in law for encouraging violence at home. 28.91 percent of the respondents blamed father in law for assaulting them. About 12.50 percent of the respondents reported abuse by their brother-in-law and 16.41 percent by their sister in-laws. Only 4.69 percent of the respondents accused relatives of victimizing them. It can thus be concluded saying domestic violence among Muslim women in Cachar District is primarily perpetrated by their husbands with or without the support of family members.

5.3.3 Duration of Domestic Violence

The respondents were interviewed on the duration of domestic violence to know how long they have been suffering from domestic violence and coping with an abusive family environment.Data has been collected accordingly and presented below (figure 5.9).

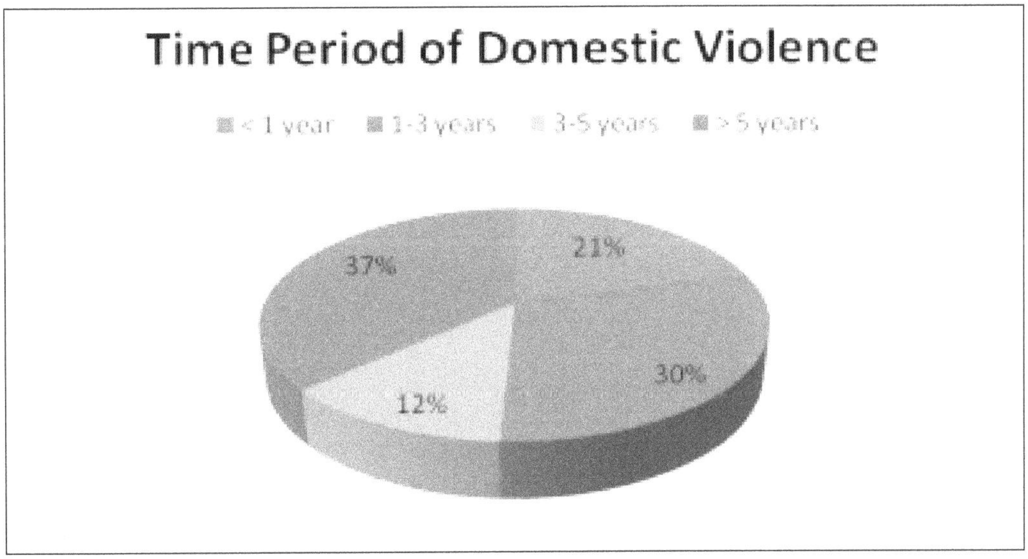

Figure 5.9: Duration of domestic Violence

The statistical information presented in the above chart reflects that the duration of facing domestic violence varies from person to person. The majority of the respondents i.e. 37 percent were facing domestic violence for more than 5 years. 30 percent have been victims for one to three years. 21percent have been victims for less than a year which explains the period immediately after marriage and 12 percent of respondents have been the victim for three to five years.

5.3.4 Factors leading to Domestic Violence

The respondents were interviewed regarding the factors that led to the violence. The responses received were in line with health factors, economic factors, sexual factors, emotional factors, and also religious factors. It has been observed that respondents had more than one factor that led to the violence.The distribution of the factors and the respondents are presented in the below table.

Table 5.3: Factors leading to domestic violence

Factors	No. of Respondents	Percentage
Health	105	82.03
Economic	66	51.56
Sexual	100	78.13
Emotional	128	100.00
Religious	117	91.40
Total	Not Applicable	Not Applicable

The statistical data exhibited in the table 5.3 shows that out of 128 respondents, 82.03 percent became victims of domestic violence for health factors. 51.56 percent of respondents reported domestic violence due to economic factors. About 78.13 percent of respondents faced domestic violence due to sexual factors and 91.41 percent were confronted with violence due to religious factors. Surprisingly all the 128 i.e. 100 percent respondents are victim of emotional factors.

5.3.5 Health Factor

Health is associated with an individual's mental state of being which is liberated from an injury or ailment. Health as a factor has a significant contribution in instigating violence against women of all sections. Many a time it is noticed that health constraints on the part of perpetrators and victims, violence at home gets increased. Thus, the study intended to identify the health issues faced by husband and wife from women's perspective. The multiple responses under health factor have been recorded and presented through a table.

Table 5.4: Health factor contributing to domestic violence

Health factors	No. of Respondents	Percentage
Suspicion of psychological disorder by abusers	13	10.15
Unable to procure children	19	14.84
Chronic health issues	28	21.87
Stress and Anxiety of husband	39	30.46
Physical deformity of husband	15	11.71
Adverse health issues of husband	42	32.81
Other	7	5.46
Total	Not Applicable	Not Applicable

The data presented above in the table 5.4shows that 10.15 percent of the respondents expressed that they were treated by abusers as mental patients while 14.84 percent of the respondents became the victim of domestic violence because of their inability to procure children. About 21.87 percent of the respondents had to suffer violence because of their chronic health issues which included diabetes, thyroid, etc. Around 30.46 percent stated that psychological problems of their husband like stress & anxiety caused violence against them at home and 11.71 percent viewed that physical limitation of husband caused violence. According to the respondents (32.81 percent), an adverse health issue of husband induces tension and mood swings which later caused violence.

5.3.6 Economic Factor

The economic factor is an important indicator of understanding women's freedom and participation in daily lives. A higher degree of work participation would increase their social prestige. But it has been observed in the study area that the majority of the respondents is economically dependent on their husbands and thus easily fall prey to domestic violence. Therefore, the study aimed to identify the economic factors leading to violence so that necessary actions can be suggested to protect women victims from violence. Accordingly, data has been collected and the following figure 5.10 presents the same.

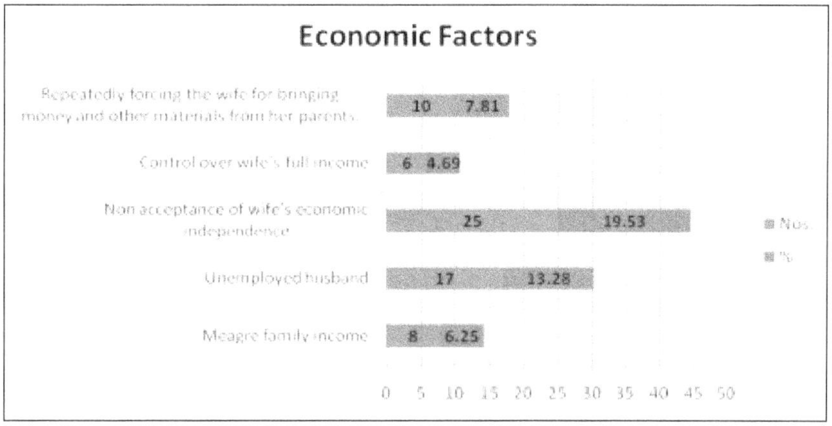

Figure 5.10: Economic factors leading to domestic violence

The economic elements that contribute to violence against Muslim women are depicted in figure 5.10. Out of 128 women surveyed, 66 (51.56 percent) believe that economic issues contributed to violence. 19.53 percent of respondents shared that their economic independence was not accepted by their husbands and those who have accepted had full control over their wife's income (4.69 percent). About 13.28 percent of the respondents said their husbands earned nothing and tried to live off their wives' income. 7.81 percent stated that their husbands' were repeatedly forcing them to get money and material from their parents and 6.25 percent of respondents reported that poor family income was one of the reasons for experiencing violence at home.

5.3.7 Sexual Factor

The sexual factor as a cause of domestic violence is hardly disclosed by the people.Previous chapters reflected that Muslim women consider it as a private matter thus doesn't prefer to bring it in public for discussion and finding out solutions. Multiple sexual factors are associated with violence against women. The following figure is presented with all information in regards to sexual factors leading to domestic violence.

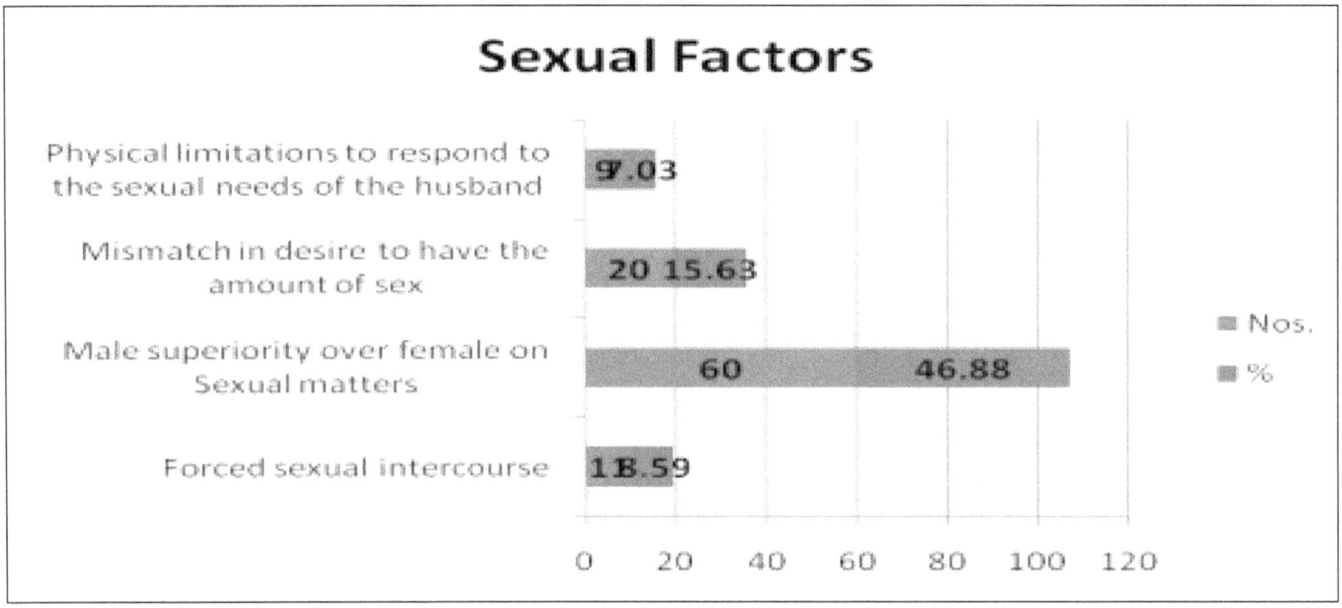

Figure 5.11: Sexual factors leading to domestic Violence

The above figure 5.11 indicates that several factors are responsible for victimizing women. Out of 128 respondents, 100 (78.13 percent) respondents reported sexual matters as a factor of domestic violence. 46.88 percent of the respondents claimed that their husband's sexual desires and demands are more important than their wife's personal preferences, and the wives must comply with their wishes even if they are uninterested. 15.63 percent said their desire for the amount of sex was out of sync. 8.59 percent complained of forced sexual intercourse, and 7.03 percent said they are unable to meet their husband's sexual desires due to physical illness or weariness, which often escalates to violence.

5.3.8 Emotional Factor

Emotion is the outcome of a strong feeling derived from one's environment, frame of mind, and relationships they have with others. Along with other factors, emotional factors played a significant role in leading to domestic violence among Muslim women of the Cachar district. All the 128 respondents have experienced violence on emotional issues. A multiple-choice question has been framed and victims were asked to share their opinion with regards to emotional factors of domestic violence. Thus the researcher recorded more than one response under each variable. The findings are presented in the following table 5.5.

Table 5.5: Emotional Factors leading to Domestic Violence

Emotional Factors	No. of Respondents	Percentage
Criticism for alleged low intelligence status	8	6.25
Humiliating for no convincing reasons	83	64.84
Scolding for expressing views on familyor financial matters	68	53.13
Repeated nagging on small and negligible matters	57	44.53
Suspecting extra marital relations	36	28.13
Restrictions in maintaining relationship with parents	13	10.16
Compelling to feel guilty for no obvious fault	25	19.53
Holding wife responsible for the ill health of kids	23	17.97
Holding wife responsible for kids poor academic performance	17	13.28
Restriction of open interaction with her children by in-laws	15	11.71
Husband's alcohol dependence	4	3.13
Total	Not Applicable	Not Applicable

The data mentioned in the above table 5.5 throws light on domestic violence for emotional factors. About twelve factors have been identified in the study under emotional aspects which have been disturbing women and making a cause of violence at home. Women find themselves in the most vulnerable situation when they experience emotional violence because such violence does not carry sound but kills one silently from inside. The data shows that the most common factor of abuse is being humiliated for no apparent cause (64.84 percent) while 53.13 percent were abused for sharing their views on family or financial matters. Around 44.53 percent of women respondents faced repeated nagging on small and negligible matters. Women were restricted to maintain the relationship with their parents (10.16 percent) and were compelled to feel guilty for no obvious fault (19.53 percent) and also they were suspected of having extramarital affairs (28.13 percent). Women were blamed for the ill health (17.97 percent) and the poor academic performance (13.28 percent) of their children. Women were not allowed to interact with their children as and when as a mother she feels like (11.71 percent). Husband's alcohol dependence (3.13 percent) and Criticism for alleged low intelligence status (6.25 percent) were also the factors of emotional violence.

5.3.9 Religious Factor

Religion is a set of beliefs and practices meant for regulating humans lives. But sometimes such beliefs and practices become a curse in society. Well, understanding holy books and changing the nature of society may lead beneficial impact on religion. It is noticed that different religious factors are leading to domestic violence. To identify these factors and to find out their association with violence, the researcher asked the respondents to share their opinion on religious factors leading to domestic violence in the Cachar district. Through multiple-choice, questions responses have been collected and more than one response under each variable has been recorded and presented in the following table 5.6.

Table 5.6: Religious factors leading to domestic violence

Religious Factors	No of Respondents	Percentage
Misinterpretation of teaching of Quran	23	17.96
Blindly following teachings of religious leaders	26	20.31
Misguided about the supremacy of men over women	39	30.46
Non adherence to traditional dresses	31	24.21
Restriction in followingmodern way of life	28	21.87
Total	Not Applicable	Not applicable

Table 5.6 depicted some of the religious elements that contribute to domestic abuse against Muslim women in families. About 30.46 percent of the respondents viewed that their husbands are misguided with the notion that men are superior to women and thus always portray authoritarian behavior. About 20.31 percent of the respondents viewed that their husbands blindly follow the teachings of religious leaders without thinking whether such teachings will yield better results or will affect further. The respondents (24.21 percent) also shared that they were abused for not covering themselves in traditional clothes and were abused for following modern culture (21.87 percent). About 17.96 percent of the respondents viewed that their husbands lack a proper understanding of the teachings of the Quran and thus they are abusing women by misinterpreting the holy Quran.

It is understood from the above discussion that there are innumerable factors influencing domestic violence against women. The study found factors like health, economic, sexual, emotional, and religious making Muslim women of the district a victim of domestic violence. These factors further led to different forms of violence against Muslim women.

5.3.10 Types of Violence faced by the Respondents

The respondents were asked to share about the violence they have experienced because of the mentioned causal factors. Physical and emotional violence were the two types of violence that have been identified during an interview with the victims which had affected the mental health of the victim from a larger perspective. The respondents stated that the violence they have experienced is varied and falls under more than one category. The following table 5.7 presents the responses.

Table 5.7: Type of Violence faced by the respondents

Type of Violence	No. of Respondents	Percentage
Physical Violence	93	72.65
Emotional Violence	128	100
Total	Not Applicable	Not Applicable

The statistical data exhibited in table 5.7 shows that out of 128 respondents 72.65 percent of respondents became victims of physical violence and 100 percent reported victims of emotional violence. This indicates that respondents are mostly abused emotionally having no sound. Other forms of violence damage the emotional well-being of the victim. Hence, it underlines the importance of addressing factors leading to emotional violence.

5.3.11 Modes of Physical Violence

To understand the nature of physical violence, the respondents were asked to share their experiences. Several alternatives were given to the respondents of which they were asked to select one or more considering their life situation and personal experiences. The below-presented table gives the details of the responses of each of the alternatives received from the respondents. The findings reveal that respondents have experienced physical violence in different forms and therefore calculated separately. As per the data collected from the respondents, 72.65 percent had been the victims of physical violence in one or another form and the analysis made on each of these forms presents the table.

Table 5.8: Mode of Physical Violence

Mode of physical violence	No. of Respondents	Percentage
Shoving roughly	88	68.75
Hurling objects towards the victim	63	49.21
Twisting arm or slapping	74	57.81
Kicking or dragging	42	32.81
Using a weapon to cause injury	38	29.68
Attempting murder	17	13.28
Total	Not Applicable	Not Applicable

Table 5.8 shows that 68.75 percent of the respondents were the victims of shoving roughly. About 57.81 percent of respondents were the victim of arm twisting and slapping while 49.21 percent were the victims of hurling with objects.About 29.68 percent reported that the abusers used weapons to cause injury to them and 32.81 percent reported being kicked and dragged out of the home. Around 13.28 percent of respondents stated that the abusers tried to murder them. Their self-esteem had been devastated by such physical assault, and they were living a life devoid of dignity.

5.3.12 Modes of Emotional Violence

Psychologists say emotional violence is more dangerous than physical violence. The injuries that take place because of physical violence may heal with time but the detrimental effects of emotional violence sustain for a long. The respondents were asked to share the emotional violence they faced. They were provided with a set of options and the freedom to have multiple choices. The responses are coded accordingly and the findings are presented below.

Table 5.9: Modes of Emotional Violence

Emotional Violence	No. of Respondents	Percentage
Threatening to divorce	23	17.96
Showing indifferent attitude towards the health of the victim	33	25.78
Threatening to commit suicide by the husband	17	13.28
Threat to use physical force	19	14.84
Threatening to remarry	24	18.75
Threatening to cast out of home	37	28.90
Threatening to harm children physically	18	14.06
Social defamation of the victim's parents	31	24.21
Total	Not Applicable	Not Applicable

The statistical presentation in table 5.9 shows that respondents were threatened to be cast out of home (28.90 percent) and abusers showed an indifferent attitude towards the health of the victim (25.78 percent). Social defamation of the parents by the abusers has emotionally weakened the victims (24.21 percent). The respondents were threatened with divorce (17.96 percent) and remarry (18.75 percent) by the abusers. The victims were given threats of experiencing physical force (14.84 percent) and to harm children physically (14.06 percent) by the abusers. There were constant threats from husbands like committing suicide (13.28 percent).

5.3.13 Immediate Reaction to Domestic Violence

It is evident from the above discussion that domestic violence is affecting women victims from all corners. Therefore, it was thought that most of the victims would have self-directed reactions to the situation. To understand the immediate reaction they were asked to choose one option from among the alternatives. On interviewing the women about the immediate feelings after being the victim of violence, they exhibited different emotions.The following table 5.10 explains the emotions:

Table 5.10: Immediate reaction to domestic violence

Reaction	No. of Respondents	Percentage
Causing self-mutilation	23	17.97
Screaming and crying	31	24.21
Breaking objects	17	13.29
Urge to leave the house	25	19.53
Feeling of helplessness	19	14.84
Urge to commit suicide	13	10.16
Total	128	100

The above table 5.10 on victims' immediate response to domestic violence reflected that 24.21 percent of the respondents burst out their anger, frustration through crying with shouts immediately after violence. About 19.53 percent of the respondents felt like leaving the house immediately after the violence and wanted to commit suicide (10.16 percent). Many a time after the violence the respondents found themselves in a helpless situation (14.84 percent) and have broken objects to manifest their anger (13.29 percent) and caused self-mutilation (17.97 percent).

5.3.14 Effects of Causal Factors on the victims

Numerable literature on domestic violence highlighted its effects on the victims. But limited studies were focused on this concerning the Cachar district. Therefore, the second objective of the study has been formulated in this direction to fill the gap of research. The study found that the casual factors have negative effects on mental health; family relations; children's wellbeing; the sexual relations and social relations of the victims. The following table 5.11 will throw light on these points.

Table 5.11: Effects of causal factors on respondents

Effects on	No. of Respondents	Percentage
Family relations	128	100
Sexual relations	73	57.03
Children's wellbeing	113	88.28
Social relations	69	53.90
Mental health	107	83.59
Total	Not Applicable	Not Applicable

The above statistical data presented in table 5.11 shows that 88.28 percent of the respondents shared that domestic violence has affected children's wellbeing; mental health (83.59%) and sexual relations (57.03 Percent) followed by social relations (53.90 percent). The data reflected that all the 128 respondents (100 percent) felt that domestic violence affected family relations specifically couple relations.

5.3.15 Effects on Family relations

The causal factors have also affected the family relations of the victims. Violence perpetrated by the husband or family members at home disturbs the conducive environment of the family and the relationship among the family members. Largely it affects the women victims of abusive behaviour at home.Therefore the study intended to ask the victims how their family life got affected due to domestic violence. They were provided with the following options and were asked to choose one or more than one. The findings showed that the victims have selected more than one option. The details about the recoded responses are presented in the following table 5.12.

Table 5.12: Effects of domestic violence on family relations

Effects on Family relations	No. of Respondents	Percentage
Marital relationship is under pressure and tension	109	85.15
Fearful family environment	33	25.78
Ignoring wife's wishes in family matters	41	32.03
Communication gap	47	36.71

Loss of mutual trust and respect	40	31.25
Conflict on minor issues	93	72.65
Family peace is destroyed	116	90.62
Total	Not Applicable	Not Applicable

The statistical presentation of the data in the above table 5.12 shows that 90.62 percent of the respondents thought that domestic violence has destroyed the peace of the family and put the marital relationship under pressure and tension (85.15 percent). Regular conflicts on minor issues (72.65 percent) and communication gap between husband-wife and in-laws led to constant misunderstandings which have disturbed the smooth functioning of the family (36.71 percent). Wife's wishes in family matters were ignored (32.03 percent) and gradually both the couples have lost mutual trust and respect (31.25 percent). The episodes of violence have made the family environment fearful (25.78 percent).

5.3.16 Effects on Sexual relations

Generally, sex is considered a private matter and so discussing it in public does not get encouragement. Therefore, sometimes it becomes difficult to put questions in this regard. It was equally difficult for the researcher to put forth questions related to sex to the women respondents. It has been noticed in the findings that husbands are always not directly perpetrating violence but indirectly instigating violence against the wife. Anger, irritation created due to violence is carried to the bedroom. In whatever way violence takes place, it affects the matrimonial relationships and as a result sex life of the victim gets affected. To identify the factors affecting sex relations, the investigator provided the following alternatives and asked to choose the options as per their choices.

Table 5.13: Effects of domestic violence on the sexual relations

Effects on sexual relations	No. of Respondents	Percentage
Diminished sexual feelings for husband	79	61.71
Decreased urge for sexual encounters	38	29.68
Sex under compulsion	52	40.62
Decline in sexual satisfaction	19	14.84
Feeling of intense repulsion on husband's sexual advance	67	52.34
Total	Not applicable	Not Applicable

The statistical presentation made in above table 5.13 on the effects of domestic violence on the sex relations of the victims reflected that the respondents have diminished their sexual feelings for their husbands (61.71 percent) and they felt disgusted on husbands' sexual advancement (52.34 percent). Sex under compulsion was another factor that affected sexual relations (40.62 percent) and the respondents (29.68 percent) have decreased urge for sexual encounters. According to the victims, there was a decline in sexual satisfaction (14.84 percent).

5.3.17 Effects on Children's wellbeing

The children, who are exposed to domestic violence, largely get affected physically and emotionally. In the study, of women who experienced domestic violence, 82 percent of them had children and they were witnessing violence. It may have a long-term impact on them. Therefore, the researcher wanted to know from the respondents in what ways violence affected their children. They were provided with the following alternatives with multiple choices. Information has been collected accordingly and presented in the following table 5.14.

Table 5.14: Effects of domestic violence on children's wellbeing

Effects on Children's wellbeing	No. of Respondents	Percentage
Poor performance in study and school	84	65.62
Difficulty in sleeping properly	42	32.81
Development of adverse traits (anxiety, fear, depression)	76	59.37
Showing aggressive/antisocial behaviour	65	50.78
Impedance in reaching developmental milestones (Speech, conversation etc)	34	26.56
Poor self esteem& self confidence	79	61.71
Total	Not Applicable	Not Applicable

The effects of domestic violence on children have been detailed in table 5.14. The statistical data reflects that domestic violence has adversely affected the performance of the children in study and school (65.62 percent). Domestic violence has also affected the self-esteem and confidence of the children (61.71 percent). The children have developed adverse traits like anxiety, fear, and depression (59.37 percent). According to the respondents, children were showing aggressive behavior on any matter (50.78 percent). Children were facing difficulty in sleeping (32.81 percent) and created impedance in reaching developmental milestones like speech, conversation, etc. (26.56 percent).

5.3.18 Effects on Social relations

Any sort of violence ends up affecting social life. As a social animal, society is the place to live in for human beings. But violence destroys the relationship of the people with society. The victims of domestic violence feel ashamed of facing society and vis-à-vis society. As a result, victims develop distance from the family &neighbors and remain within themselves which weakens the victim from inside. The study intended to understand in what way domestic violence is affecting victims and thus were asked to share their opinion by selecting options of their choice from among the multiple alternatives.

Table 5.15: Effects of domestic violence on social relations

Effects on Social relations	No. of Respondents	Percentage
Limited communication with family	26	20.31
Ashamed of facing neighbors	39	30.46
Avoidance of social gathering	28	21.87
Lost contact with relatives, friends	34	26.56
Facing social isolation	18	14.06
Social defamation of victim's family members	23	17.96
Total	Not Applicable	Not Applicable

The above table 5.15 shows that 30.46 percent of the respondents were ashamed of facing neighbors. They were even afraid to show their faces because of the sounds of screaming and assaults at home. The respondents' families were looked upon differently by the society and thus had to face social isolation by 14.06 percent. About 26.56 percent of the respondents have lost connectivity with friends and relatives because they did not want to damage their relatives and friends by telling them the truth. About 20.31 percent had limited communications with her family members as she was not allowed to maintain communication by the abusers and 21.87 percent had stopped attending social functions. Around 17.96 percent of the respondents had to face social defamation of their parents in society which affected their mental health severely.

5.3.19 Effects on Mental Health

Different studies have concluded that women who are exposed to domestic abuse are relatively prone to mental health problems. They suffer from anxiety, depression and suicidal thoughts, etc. (Brandi Walker 2020). Studies have also shown that 30-60% of women with mental health issues are likely to experience domestic violence (Howard,

L.M., Trevillion, K. et.al 2009) and such situations have detrimental effects on woman's overall emotional and mental health. Therefore, the present study intended to understand the mental health status of the women who are victims of domestic violence. Thus, they were given options and asked to choose one or more from among them. The recorded data reflected that the respondents have chosen more than one emotion and thus it came to 369 responses.

Table 5.16: Effects of domestic violence on mental health

Mental Health	No. of Respondents	Percentage
Under constant stress	88	68.75
Severe anxiety and depression	67	52.34
Frequent mood swings	46	35.93
Sleep disturbance	81	63.28
Suicidal tendency	33	25.78
Increased lethargy and fatigability	54	42.18
Total	Not Applicable	Not Applicable

The statistical presentation of the data in the above table 5.16 shows that 68.75 percent of the respondents are subject to constant mental stress and 63.28 percent are a victim of sleep disturbance. About 52.34 percent of the respondents reported their feeling of hopelessness and anxiety.42.18 percent developed lethargy and fatigability followed by frequent mood swings by 35.93 percent of the respondents. The study reported that 25.78 percent of respondents expressed their suicidal tendencies.

5.4 Help seeking approach of the Respondents

5.4.1 Help Sought by the respondents

The investigator wanted to know after being exposed to violence followed by severe effects on victims how the victims have coped with the situation and whether they have approached anybody for seeking support; if, yes, whom did they approach. With all these questions in mind, the investigator asked the respondents to share their responses by choosing options given as multiple choices. The responses revealed that the respondents expressed more than one feeling which is presented in the following figure 5.12.

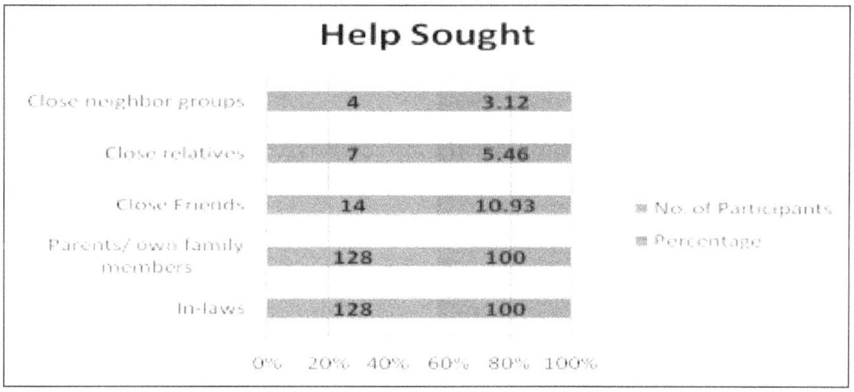

Figure 5.12: Help Sought by the respondents

The above figure 5.12 shows that all the 128 respondents have sought help from their in-laws and parents. Despite knowing the fact that in many cases in-laws are themselves the creator of violence yet 100 percent of the respondents approached in-laws for helping out them from the crisis and the same population approached (100 percent) their parents too. About 10.93 percent have sought guidance from their childhood friends and 5.46 percent approached close relatives of both sides (in-laws & own) on whom they can trust. Only 3.12 percent shared their problems with close neighbors and sought help. The data reveals that though women are falling prey to violence because of husbands' family members yet they did hope to get support from them. Victims are found equally dependent on their parents and thus their social image became a matter of concern for them.

5.4.2 Help received by the respondent from the Families

The above findings revealed that 100 percent of the respondents sought help from their in-laws and parents to overcome the situation. The findings further made a scope to understand how far the victims have received help from in-laws and parents. Therefore, they were asked to share their experiences in the light of support received from the mentioned group of people for resolving the problem. Information has been gathered accordingly and presented in the following table 5.17

Table 5.17: Help received from the families

Help Received	No. of Respondents		Total
	Yes	No	
Husbands Family	11 (8.59%)	117 (91.40%)	128 (100%)
Victims Family	121 (94.53%)	7 (5.46%)	128 (100%)

The above table 5.17 shows that 91.40 percent of the respondents stated that there was no effort made by the husband's family for resolving the conflicting situation rather they were the creators of the problem and only 8.59 percent of the respondents received support from the husband's family to resolve the conflict, as reported by the respondents. On another side, 5.46 percent of the respondents stated that they have not received any support from their parents whereas 94.53 percent of the respondents have received support, guidance and advice from their parents to get rid of the abusive situation.

5.4.3 Suggestions given by the parents of Victims

It has been understood from the above data that the respondents have received more guidance and support from their parents rather than husbands family. Therefore, the respondents were asked to share about the measures or advices suggested by their parents.Their responses were recorded and presented in a figure form.

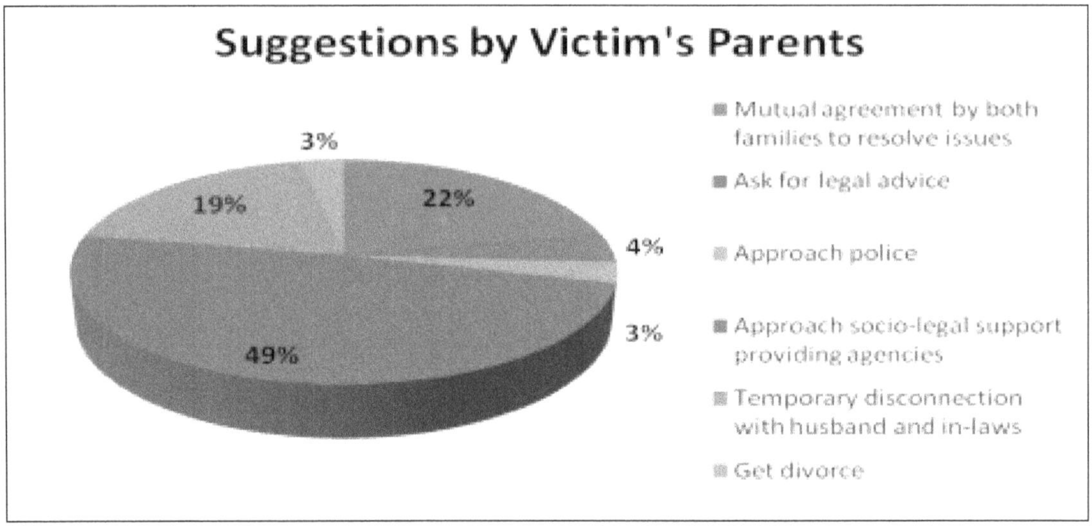

Figure 5.13: Measures suggested by victims' parents

The statistical presentation of the data made on figure 5.13 reveals that 49 percent of the respondents were suggested to approach socio-legal support providing agencies working on domestic violence issues and register their cases. 22 percent of the respondents were suggested to rethink the issues leading to violence and give another try for restoring the relationship by mutual agreement. About 19 percent of the respondents were advised to maintain disconnection with husband and in-laws temporarily and 4 percent were suggested with seeking legal consultations. Breaking up or getting divorced or reporting to the police was the least prevalent type of advice, accounting for 3 percent respectively. This explains why Muslim women are still terrified of ending their relationships or reporting abusive partners to the authorities.

5.5 Reporting of Cases

5.5.1 Organizations approached for reporting of cases by the respondents

After getting the suggestions, it was interesting to see how many of the victims could act as per the suggestion given by their parents while staying at in-laws house. Majority (49 percent) of the parents suggested them to seek socio-legal services from both Government and Non Government Organizations and register their cases. Therefore, the respondents were asked to share the organizations that they approached for further help and support. It was interesting to see in the study that the respondents have approached both Government and social organizations for seeking support. Respondents who were advised to get divorce and stay disconnected for some time have also approached different organizations for registering their cases. The information collected in this regard is presented in the following table 5.18.

Table 5.18: Organizations approached for reporting of cases

Organisation Approached	No. of Respondents	Percentage
Police Department	19	14.85
Family Court	24	18.76
Panchayat	36	28.12
District Court	18	14.06
District Social Welfare department	17	13.28
Social organizations	14	10.93
Total	128	100

Among the mentioned organizations in table 5.18, Panchayat has recorded the highest number of cases as informed by the respondents (28.12 percent). About 18.75 percent approached the family court and 14.84 percent reported their cases to the police department and 14.06 percent to the district court. About 13.28 percent approached district social welfare for reporting of the cases and only 10.93 percent approached social organizations. It is clear from the data that Panchayat plays a crucial role in providing assistance to Muslim women that are victims of abusive behavior at home.

5.5.2 Services sought from the approached organizations

The investigator wanted to know the type of services respondents were expecting from the approached organizations and how far they were provided with such services.

Table 5.19: Services sought from the approached organizations

Services sought for	No of Respondents	Percentage
Family counseling	38	29.7
Rescue	24	18.75
Shelter	43	33.59
legal assistance	23	17.96
Total	128	100

Table 5.19 shows that 33.59 percent of the respondents were seeking shelter service and 29.7 percent of the respondents desperately wanted external help to counsel their family members so that violence on daily basis gets solved. About 18.75 percent shared, they were looking for rescue services as they didn't get help from anybody at the time of violence to come and rescue them. About 17.96 percent were seeking legal guidance to stay alert. According to the respondents, none of the organizations could provide comprehensive support services to the victims.

5.5.3 Intervention by the Organizations Approached

The study wanted to understand how far approached organizations and departments could intervene victim's problems. Therefore, respondents were asked to share their experiences of receiving services from them in the form of yes or no. Through this question, an attempt has also been made to understand how far approached organizations could satisfy the respondents with their responses and services. It was expected by the respondents that approached organizations would render their services in the form of registering cases, family counselling, rescue, shelter, and legal assistance

Table 5.20: Intervention by the organisations approached

Intervention by the approached Organization	No. of respondents	Percentage
Yes	56	43.75
No	72	56.25
Total	128	100

It is understood from Table 5.20 that the majority of the respondents (56.25 percent) were not satisfied with the intervention made by the approached organization and 43.75 percent of the respondents expressed that the organizations could partially solve their problems. Respondents of both the category (yes/no) reported that none of the organizations had a comprehensive support service mechanism for the victims of domestic violence. According to them they could register their case but faced problems in continuing with the case because of lengthy official procedures. Some organizations have reported the case but later referred to another organization and they have followed up the case. The study found that even after reaching out to formal groups only 17 percent were provided with individual counseling services and 17.96 percent provided with legal services. About 59 percent provided with services like home visits, referral, connecting with the social organizations while 75 percent of the respondents have not received any services. Rather they were suggested to register with formal social organizations that advocate for the rights of the victim of domestic violence. They were also told that approaching such organizations would make the entire process of filing a complaint against the abuser would be easy and smooth, as reported by the respondents. Even more than 90 percent of the respondents were ready to approach organizations exclusively working on domestic violence issues and offering services as per the need of the victim.

5.6 Awareness about Support Providing Agencies

5.6.1 Awareness status

The respondents were advised to register their cases with social support providing agencies to ensure comprehensive services. Therefore, it was interesting to know how far the victims were aware about the organizations and the type of services provided by such organizations. The responses have been recorded in the form of yes and no and are presented in the following figure.

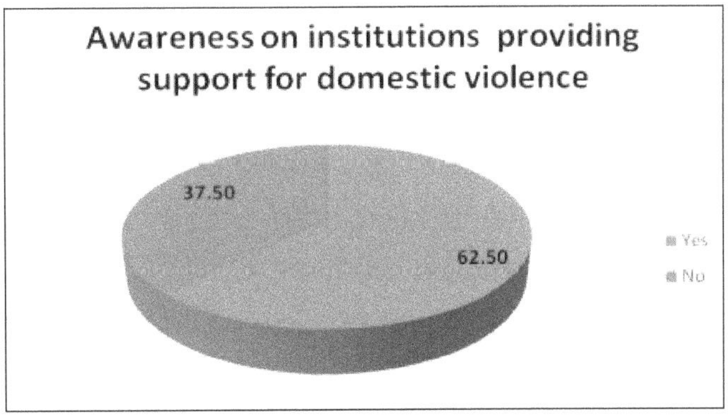

Figure 5.14: Awareness about support providing agencies

According to figure 5.14, about 62.50 percent of the respondents were aware about the support providing agencies but not about their functions in details and 37.50 percent of the respondents were unaware about such support providing organizations. According to the respondents initially they have not had much information about these organisations but gradually from parents & family members (43%), Government officials (27%), Friends (4%), Newspaper (6%), and Local clubs (20%), they came to know about the support providing agencies and subsequently sought help from them.

5.6.2 Support providing agencies approached for registration of cases

Social organizations are rooted in society. They work for the development of the individual, group, and community with specific support services. They play different roles in the society like identifying social issues, addressing such issues with modern tools and techniques to provide a better future to the vulnerable section of the population. Therefore, it was interesting to see in the study whether the Muslim women victims have approached social organizations as per the suggestion given by the professionals. It was found that the respondents have approached three organizations who have been working on domestic violence issues for a quite long time in the district. The detail of which is presented in the following figure.

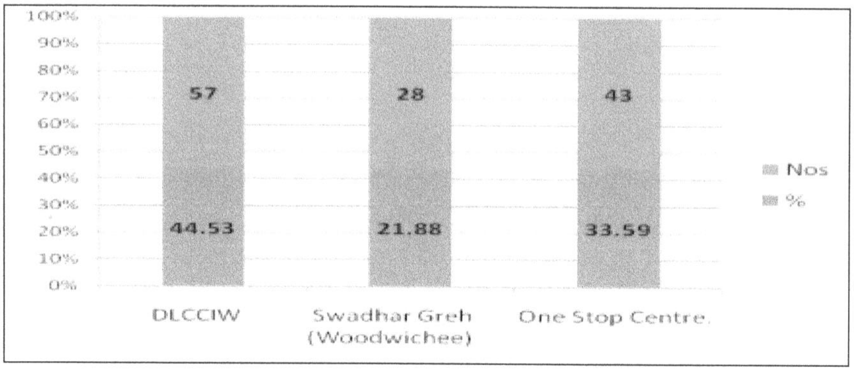

Figure 5.15: Agencies approached for registration of cases

The above figure 5.15 reflects that all 128 victims reached out to the District level committee for a crime involving women (DLCCIW), SwadharGreh of Woodwichee organization, and One Stop Centre for registering and seeking assistance. The statistical presentation of the data reveals that 44.53 percent of the respondents sought support services from DLCCIW and 21.88 percent from the SwadharGreh followed by 35.59 percent from one stop centre. This explains why these three organizations are the most well-known in Cachar for helping victims of domestic violence.

5.7 Services provided by the support providing agencies

The mentioned three organizations were with different support services for the victims of domestic violence. One-Stop Centres (OSCs) are intended to help women who are the victim of brutalities in both public and private spheres as well as in a home, community, and workplace. Women getting through physical, sexual, psychological, and economic abuse are provided with support and redressal services irrespective of their age, class, rank, race, culture, or educational and conjugal status. The SwadharGreh scheme aims to provide transitory accommodation to women in need by establishing an institutional framework that empowers them and ensures that they have access to critical support services. It envisions such women having access to housing, food, clothing, and health care, as well as economic and social security. DLCCIW provides counselling and legal aid services.

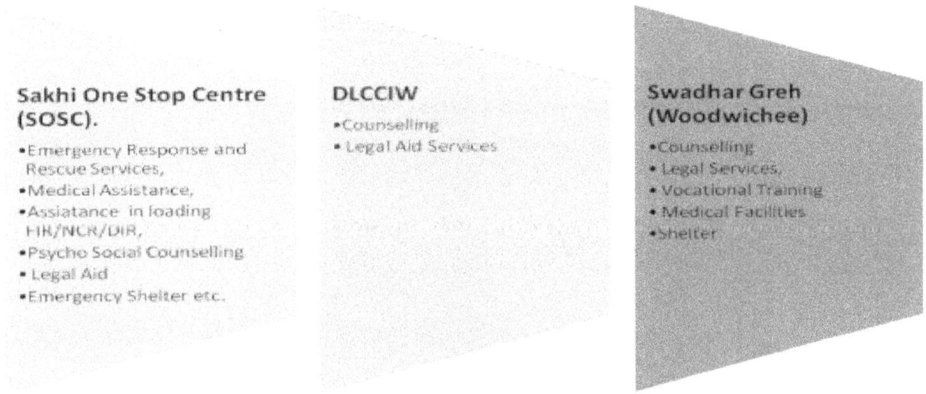

Diagram5.1: Services provided by the support providing agencies

5.7.1 Support Services Received by the Respondents

Since a good number of services of different nature are provided to the women victims of domestic violence by the support providing agencies, so it was important to see whether respondents have received all the services or the specific few services as per the need. Therefore the respondents were asked to share their experiences about the services received. It was found that in some cases respondents were provided with more than one service. Their responses are presented below in table no. 5.21.

Table 5.21: Support services received by the respondents

Services	No. of Respondents	Percentage
Emergency Response and Rescue Services	15	11.71
Medical Assistance	17	13.28
Assistance in lodging FIR	8	6.25
Psycho-social support/ counselling	81	63.28
Legal aid and counselling	58	45.31

Shelter	35	27.34
Vocational training	24	18.75
Total	Not applicable	Not Applicable

The above table 5.21 is clear to understand that the three organizations have provided a variety of services. Only counselling support services were received by 63.28 percent of the respondents. About 45.31 percent have received legal aid counselling and 27.34 percent have availed shelter services. 13.28 percent of the respondents have received medical assistance and 18.75 percent have received vocational training. 11.71 percent were provided with emergency response and rescue services and 6.25 percent were provided with assistance in lodging FIR.

5.7.2 Problems faced by the respondents in receiving services

The above discussion revealed that the Muslim women respondents have availed different services under different organizations. Therefore, the study intended to know whether the respondents have faced any difficulty in receiving such services. Accordingly, they were asked to share their opinion if they have faced any problem in availing support services. Another purpose of asking this question was to understand whether the service delivery mechanism is victim-oriented or not. The responses received are presented through the following figure.

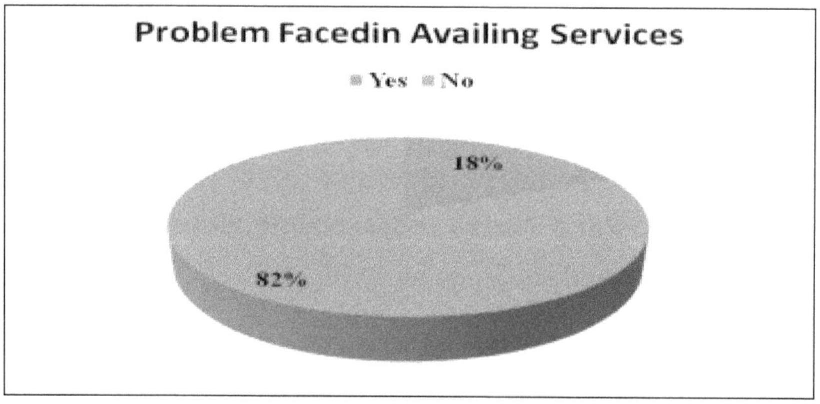

Figure 5.16: Problem faced in availing the services

Figure 5.16depicts that 82 percent of the respondents expressed that they have not faced any difficulty in receiving the services while 18 percent showed little dissatisfaction and said they encountered challenges in availing services. According to them the procedure of dealing with the cases was lengthy and attending a series of counseling sessions was a problematic one. Convincing the husband for the session and coming out from the home always was not in favour of the victims. In some situations, they were not heard properly by the legal consultants and had to experience neglect attitude by the office-bearers.

5.7.3 Support providing agencies in problem solving

It is not always possible that all given services will yield a positive result. But it is expected such services will have a certain impact on the lives of the victims. Therefore, the respondents were interviewed regarding the extent to which the services offered could solve their problem. The responses are recorded below in figure 5.17.

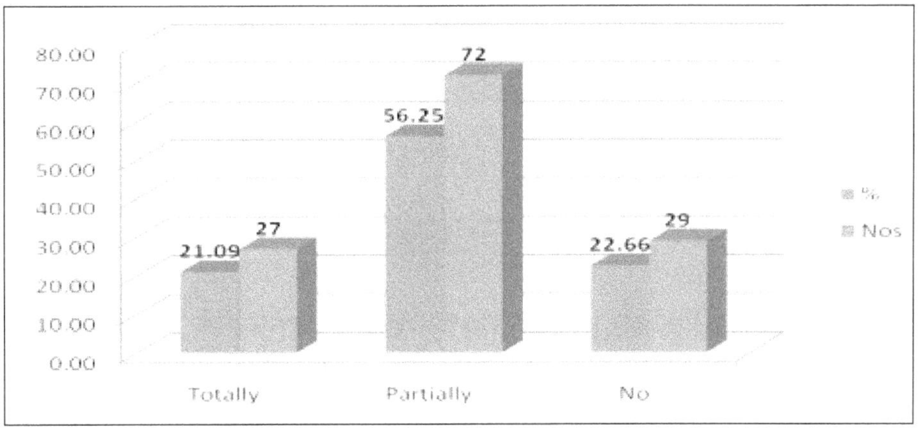

Figure 5.17: Support providing agencies in problem solving

Figure 5.17explains that no matter all the organizations were offering services and all the respondents have registered for help, only 21.09% claimed that they could end their problem totally while 56.25% claimed that the services could solve their problem partially and 22.66% claimed that their problems persist and the services by these organizations could not bring a satisfactory result. For 56.25% who claimed that their problems were solved partially had given the following reasons:

1. The legal assistance supplied was insufficient to put an end to the battles.
2. The victims were not given adequate assistance in obtaining custody of their children.
3. The victims were not assisted in obtaining monetary support from their husbands.
4. The procedure was slow and failed to meet the deadline.

Alternatives to Unsolved Problems

The above statistics revealed that 22.65 percent of the respondents (29) were still with the problems. Therefore it was important to know what other alternatives they have adopted to cope with the problematic situation. The study recorded numerous responses that are presented below in table 5.22.

Table 5.22: Alternatives to unsolved problems

Alternatives	No. of Respondents	Percentage
Living with husband's family and compromising with the situation	21	16.40
Living with parents and trying to restart life	4	3.12
Living alone and working	3	2.34
Reached out to different organisation for seeking support	1	0.79
Total	29	22.65

Table 5.22 shows that even after approaching formal organisation the respondents remained with problems. About 16.40 percent of respondents shared that they went back to living with their husbands and compromising with the situation and 3.12 percent went back to living with parents and trying to restart their lives. Around 2.34 percent started living alone and working hard for their sustainability and only 0.79 percent again approached other organizations for seeking help.

5.8 Perception of the Respondents about the Services Provided

5.8.1 Satisfaction level about the services provided

The above discussion on problems faced in receiving the services and solving the problems highlighted that 18% of respondents faced problems in receiving services and 22.65% of respondents are still with the problems. Despite the mentioned problems, the investigator made an effort to understand the overall satisfaction level of the respondents about the services provided by the support providing agencies. The recorded responses are presented in the following figure.

Figure 5.18: Satisfaction level of the respondents on the services received

Despite having problems and challenges in receiving the services and solving the problems, 88 percent (113) of the respondents expressed their satisfaction with the services received, according to chart 7.3. The services were unsatisfactory to 12 percent (15) of the respondents.

5.8.2 Service Components which satisfied the respondents

The above data reflects that 88 percent of the respondents were satisfied with the services provided to them. Therefore, they were asked to share the service components which made them satisfied. The recorded responses are presented in below table.

Table 5.23: Services which satisfied the respondents

Service components	No. of Respondents	Percentage
Psycho-social support and Counselling	74	57.81
Legal Aid	11	8.59
Shelter	21	16.40
Vocational training	7	5.46
Total	113	88.26

Table 5.23 indicates that 57.81 percent of the respondents expressed their satisfaction with counselling services provided by the organization. According to them counselling has improved their sense of wellbeing, alleviated distressing feelings, and boosted mental health. Counselling helped them to understand their problems and associated environmental factors. It has helped the respondents to make an assessment of the symptoms causing psychological problems, diagnose the symptoms and find out ways as part of treatment. About 16.40 percent of respondents expressed satisfaction with the shelter component of the

services provided. The shelter is one of the survival needs of the human being. The previous discussion highlighted that victims had no place to stay even for a night which compelled them to live in the abusive family. Through this shelter home service at least victims have got a place to take shelter immediately after violence. Due to financial constraints many of the respondents could not afford legal fees thus have not received any legal guidance. But free legal aid services of the organization have helped the victims to fight with their cases and get them solved which made them happy and satisfied too (8.59 respondents).About 5.46 percent of the respondents expressed satisfaction with vocational training. Economic dependence was one of the factors of violence against Muslim women. Under that backdrop when women were provided with vocational training, especially at SwadharGreh was not less than a blessing to them. According to the respondents it has given them an opportunity for skill-building and becoming economically self-sufficient.

5.8.3 Service component which dissatisfied the respondents

There were 12 percent (15) of the respondents who expressed dissatisfaction on certain components and these are as follows in the table 5.24

Table 5.24: Services which dissatisfied the respondents

Service components	No. of Respondents	Percentage
Legal Aid Counselling	6	4.68
Rescue	4	3.12
Vocational Training	5	3.90
Total	15	11.7

According to table 5.24, about 4.68 percent of the respondents expressed dissatisfaction with the legal aid counselling component. According to them, for more than a week they have not got legal help nor did receive psycho-social counselling. After waiting for long they have attended legal aid counselling sessions for once only and after that no such counselling was provided to them and thus their problems remained unsolved.

About 3.12 percent of the respondents were dissatisfied with the rescue service component. According to them, they have made calls to the organization at the time of crises and distress but none from the organization have come to rescue the victim. According to 3.90 percent of the respondents, vocational training is an important component as it could help the victim to earn a livelihood. Training on tailoring was provided but the victims were not provided with raw materials for undergoing such training and therefore they had to purchase raw materials from their own money and became factor dissatisfied.

5.8.4 Compelling Reasons for Staying in Abusive Relationship

It was evident from the data that the women respondent had a series of episodes of violence, yet the majority of them were in marital relationships. Therefore the researcher intended to know the reasons which compel them to stay in an abusive relationship where there is no care, love & respect. Hence, the respondents of all categories (married, separated, divorce, widow) were approached to share the reasons that force a woman to go on with the harmful relationship or split the difference with the circumstance. The responses received are varied in nature and presented in the following table 5.25.

Table 5.25: Compelling reasons for staying in an abusive relationship

Compelling Reasons	No. of Respondents	Percentage
No alternative house to stay	21	16.41
Children's future	68	53.12
Parents repute	26	20.31
Hoping for better future	13	10.16
Total	128	100

In accordance to the table 5.25, majority of the Muslim women (53.12 percent) have continued with the abusive relationship thinking about kid's future. About 20.31 percent compromised with the situation to safeguard the reputation of their parents while 16.40 percent had surrendered before the circumstance because of not having an alternate place to stay and only 10.15 percent were in the abusive relationship hoping to have a better tomorrow.

5.8.5 Suggestions for reducing Domestic Violence by the Respondents

All through the interactions, the respondents were very enthusiastic and were providing information to the best of their efforts. Thus, it was thought necessary to get their suggestion to reduce domestic violence, and therefore following alternatives were given and were asked to choose one or more than one option as part of their suggestion.

Table 5.26: Suggestions for reducing domestic violence by respondents

Suggestion	No. of Respondents	Percentage
Creating mass awareness on domestic violence issues at family and community level	93	72.65
Creating awareness about the support service providing agencies at the community level	86	67.18

Strict implementation of the laws meant for protecting victims	74	57.81
Active involvement of Social workers & NGOs & local governance	42	32.81
Programme on promoting healthy marital relationships	18	14.06
Total	Not Applicable	Not Applicable

The above table 5.26 shows that the majority of the respondents i.e. 72.65 percent (93) felt that there is a dearth of awareness and thus suggested creating awareness about domestic violence issues at the family and community level. Adding to that further 67.18 percent of the respondents shared about creating awareness about the support service providing agencies at the community level so that the vulnerable women get the benefit. About 57.81 percent expressed that there is a law to punish the abusers yet in some cases they are not being given punishment and move freely in the society, so they suggested strict implementation of the laws meant for protecting the women victims. Besides that, 32.81 percent suggested for active involvement of social workers, NGOs, and local governance for launching a drive against domestic violence. 14.06 percent of the respondents suggested organizing sessions or programs on promoting healthy marital relationships.

5.9 Problems faced by the support providing agencies in delivering their services to the victims of Domestic Violence in Cachar District of Assam

Since the study was focused on Muslim women so it was likewise important to investigate whether there are any cultural reservations on the part of the organization in terms of service providing. Accordingly, the fourth objective was formulated to understand the difficulties encountered by the service providing agencies in delivering services to a Muslim women victim.

5.9.1 Profile of the organisation

5.9.1.1 Sakhi One Stop Centre

Background of the organisation

The gang rape and murder of a 23-year-old physiotherapy student in Delhi on December 16, 2012, incited cross-country shock. Subsequently, Nirbhaya Fund was set up in 2013 to help women impacted by violence. It is under this backdrop, the Union government had proposed the foundation of One-stop centres that would give temporary shelter, guidance for registering complaints, and facilitates them with needed medical, legal, and psychological assistance. The centre is planned to help women impacted by brutality in the family, local area and at work. Women confronting physical, sexual, emotional, psychological, maltreatment regardless of their age, position, marital status, culture etc. Distressed ladies confronting any sort of brutality because of endeavored inappropriate behavior, rape, abusive behavior at home, dealing, honor-related wrongdoings, corrosive assaults, or witch-hunting who have connected or been alluded to the OSC will be furnished with specific servicess.

➢ *Objectives of the organisation*

i) To provide integrated support and assistance to women affected by violence, both in private and public spaces under one roof.

ii) To facilitate immediate, emergency, and non-emergency access to a range of services including medical, legal, psychological, and counselling support under one roof to fight against any forms of violence against women.

➢ *Organisational Structure*

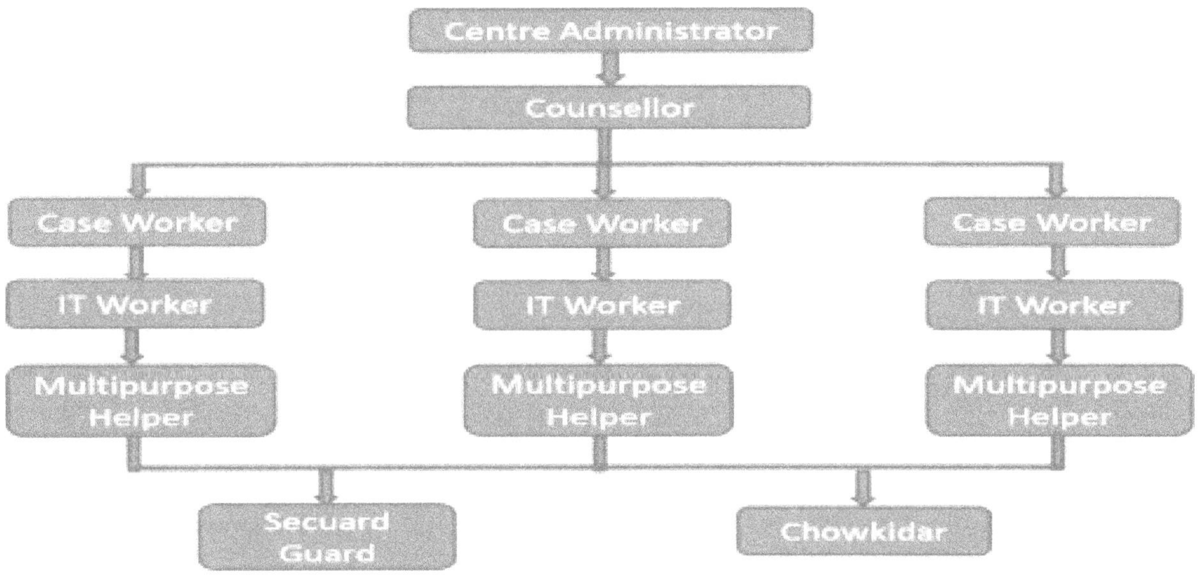

Diagram 5.2: Organisational structure of Sakhi One Stop Centre

Sources of Fund

The one stop centre is a centrally funded programme which further provides full financial assistance to state government/ union territories. The respective state governments provides fund to District Commissioner and the District Commissioner provides fund to organization who implement the scheme at the district level. In Cachar, the centre is run by Paradise NGO selected by the District administration.

5.9.1.2 District Level Committee for Crime Involving Women (DLCCIW)

➢ *Background of the Organisation*

The Committee was set up by the Deputy Commissioner, Cachar, Assam vide office notice No.CCL.25/9742, dated-20/05/1997 with a view to exercises and reasonably sharpen different issues looked at by the women. On 15th August 1997, the Committee in the court compound close to SaniMandir was established d by the then Hon'ble Minister for Rural Development Mr.SahidulAlamChoudhury in the presence of an august gathering. A woman might be associated with a specific case enlisted in a police headquarters as a charged or a complainant or a casualty of an offense. Much of the time because of ignorance and destitution the women are not in a situation to get appropriate justice from the existing system. Quite often they are also not aware of the legal safeguards available to them and they do not get proper guidance at the right time. The primary motivation behind the Committee is to find all potential ways to kill different sorts of violations being committed against women which have expanded at a threatening rate in the District of Cachar, Assam.

➢ *Objective of the organisation*

The main objectives of the District Level Committee for Crime Involving Women (DLCCIW) are as follows:

i) To coordinate with the Deputy Commissioner, Superintendent of Police & District level functionaries of Cachar District of Assam for dealing with issues relating to women and monitor their cases.

ii) To take up possible measures for curbing crime against women in collaboration with police stations.

iii) To take extreme care of the clients so that investigations in cases involving crimes against women are not being hampered.

iv) To arrange a mass awareness programme about the legal rights of women in various parts of the district.

v) To arrange family counseling in the office of the Committee and look into the matter of allegation or complaint made by the women.

vi) To provide help and guidance to women under distress and assist them in taking legal actions.

vii) To extend all possible help to women made accused in a case at the inquiry stage, as well as in the trial stage.

viii) To make regular visits to the District jail to see the condition of women convict or women UTP in the Jail.

ix) To extend help to the police for the safe custody of women if any women are required to be kept custody other than the police station.

x) To coordinate with other organizations working for the cause of women.

Organisational Structure

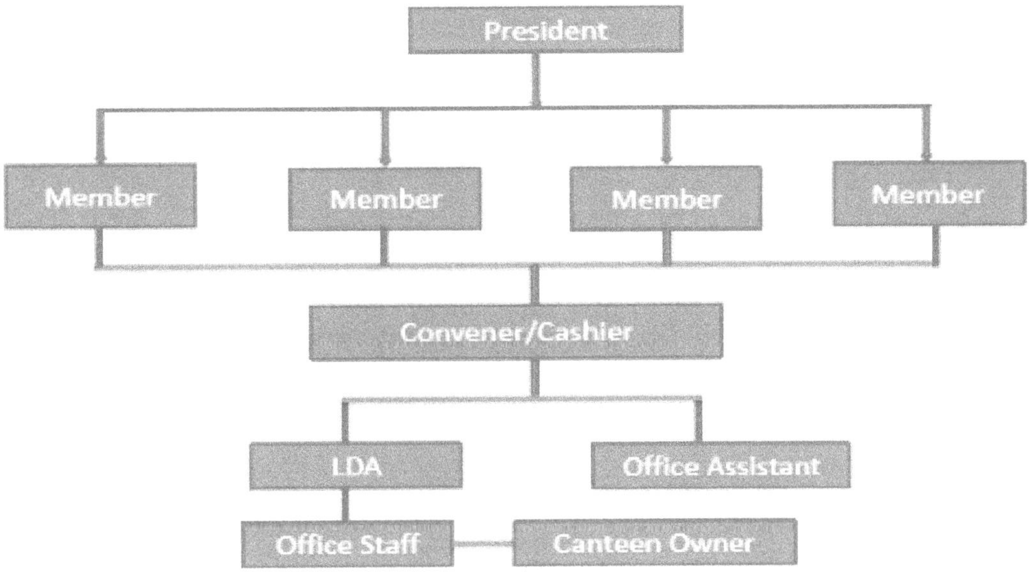

Diagram 5.3: Organisational structure of DLCCIW

Sources of Fund

The only source of funds is registration fees. The organization collects Rs. 200/- as case registration fees from the complainant. The accumulated amount is spent for maintenance of the organization along with the salary of the staff.

5.9.1.3 SwadharGreh

➢ *Background of the organisation*

The Government of India has been executing various plans to give safe house to ladies deprived beginning around 1969. Understanding the requirement for temporary safe house, the Ministry of Women and Child Development has presented the SwadharGreh conspire. The SwadharGreh plot was the result of two consolidated plans named swadhar and short-

remain at home (SSH). The objective of the combined plan is all ladies survivors of awful conditions as well as ladies in trouble, including widows, down and out ladies, and matured ladies. The plan offers advantages to youngsters going with ladies of referenced classes. The plan gives brief private convenience, food, clothing, clinical offices, professional and expertise up-degree preparing, advising, and legitimate guide to ladies in trouble.

➤ *Objective of the organisation*

i) To cater to the primary need of shelter, food, clothing, medical treatment and care of women in distress, and *those* who are without any social and economic support.
ii) To enable them to regain their emotional strength that gets hampered due to their encounter with unfortunate circumstances.
iii) To provide them with legal aid and guidance to enable them to take steps for their readjustment in family/society.
iv) To rehabilitate them economically and emotionally.
v) To act as a support system that understands and meets various requirements of women in distress.
vi) To enable them to start their life afresh with dignity and conviction.

➤ *Organisational Structure*

Diagram 5.4 Organisational structure of SwadharGreh

Sources of fund

The SwadharGreh scheme is sponsored by the Ministry of Women & Child Development. Therefore, the main source of funding is Government. The Central government sanctions fund to state government and the state government to District Commissioner and the district commissioner sanctions and releases funds to the concerned organization at the district level. In Cachar, Wodwichee, (NGO) is implementing the scheme. Thus, to implement the scheme smoothly, Wodwichee has been receiving funds from the District administration.

5.10 Type of Cases Registered in the organisation

These organizations keep track of a variety of instances. Some cases are taken because of the distance between the parties involved, while others are initiated to take advantage of specific services. However, the study discovered that cases are reported from a variety of religions and hence cannot be classified as religious. The following diagram depicts the many types of cases that are brought.

Diagram 5.5: Cases dealt by Service Providers

While domestic violence cases are commonplace across all organizations, SOSC, in addition, focuses on human trafficking and kidnapping, DLCCIW also concentrates on property-related issues, and SwadharGreh emphasizes providing shelter to fewer victims of domestic violence.

5.10.1 Process of Dealing with the cases

A common process for dealing with the cases is not followed. Different cases follow different methods. The present study is on domestic violence so the process of dealing with such cases will be discussed here.

5.10.1.1 Sakhi One Stop Centre

To deal with domestic violence cases the following process are followed by the one-stop centre.

- *Emergency Response & Rescue service*

    1. The center receives cases directly or through 181 toll-free number
    2. If the case is received through 181, immediately the center informs the nearest police station
    3. The center starts contacting the victims and coordinating with the police.
    4. To verify the genuinity of the case, Police sometimes ask someone from the victim's family to file a complaint in the police station or center.
    5. Sometimes victim's party do respond and sometimes not
    6. Understanding the gravity of the case the police team goes for rescuing the victim.
    7. If the case is received directly by the Centre, then immediately they contact with nearest police station of the victim, the rescue team visits the victim's house and discusses the matter. The victim is asked what she wants to do.

- *Emergency Shelter*

    1. After rescue they are given temporary shelter to a one-stop center for 5 days.
    2. If their stay becomes required for more than 5 days then on special permission from Deputy Commissioner, Cachar, an additional 5 days can be expanded. After that, these victims are referred to Ujjawala and SwadharGreh's home.

- *Psycho Social Support Counseling*

    1. Within this timeframe case history is taken and required counseling is given.
    2. If required home visit and interaction with the neighbors is done for further data collection
    3. Based on the collected data, analysis is made and looks for victims wish.
    4. If victim is interest to undergo counseling session then she is provided with.
    5. If required with her consent, husband and family members are called for attending counseling sessions.

6. Depending upon the nature of cases counseling sessions are arranged as per the convenience of the service receiver and provider.

- *Medical Assistance*

  Within these 5 days medical check-up of the victim is done in medical college if the case is brought by the police and if the case is directly addressed by the centre then the medical checkup is done by them in civil hospital, Cachar, Silchar.

- *Assistance in Lodging FIR*

  1. If the victim wants to file FIR, the centre coordinates with the police and
  2. If the victim does not want to file FIR and wants to solve the problem through mutual discussion then the centre arranges a meeting with her husband and family members in the centre.
  3. The centre also assists victims to file complaints against abusers in family court for divorce and maintenance.

- *Legal Assistance*

  If the victim wants to take legal advice then she is made connected with DLSA for free legal advice. The One Stop Centre has also empanelled lawyers. They are called for providing legal counselling by the center for the victims. Sometimes legal counselling session is arranged at the center itself or in the bar association.

5.10.1.2 District Level Committee for Crime Involving Women (DLCCIW)

The process of dealing with domestic violence cases in DLCCIW is as follows:

- *Emergency Response*

  1. The agency does not have a rescue service but does respond the cases immediately after coming to the agency.
  2. The first thing that the agency does is make registration of the case. For this, the victim has to fill up a registration form with a minimal fee of Rs. 230/-.
  3. The basic demographic profile is collected and initiates an interactive process with the motive to offer a friendly environment to the victims.
  4. Once rapport is built the client is asked to narrate her story and thereby case history of the client is collected and studied carefully.
  5. The client is asked to share her opinion. If the client wants to reconcile then a notice is sent to the offender party for appearing before the committee.
  6. Offender party gets a chance to present their views about the case registered.

7. If they want to solve the problem mutually then through counseling sessions problem is solved. And if they wish for legal advisers, they are made connected accordingly.

- *Counseling*

1. Initially victim is counseled and in the second phase counseling is done with the families and in the third phase, both the parties are brought face to face.
2. The severity of the case determines the counseling session.
3. During counseling sessions surprise visits are given by the organization to the victim's house to monitor their activities.
4. If everything is found favorable the counseling sessions will be terminated.

- *Medical Assistance*

The DLCCIW does not provide Medical Assistance services but makes a referral of such cases to Silchar Medical College, Civil Hospital. In the case of affluent families, the referral is done to private hospitals also.

- *Assistance to women in lodging FIR/ NCR/DIR*

The DLCCIW directly do not provide assistance in terms of lodging FIR. But shares the sources from where they can get better services.

- *Shelter*

The DLCCIW does not provide shelter services to the victims. But if the organization feels, the victim requires shelter then she is referred and made connections with other organizations providing shelter services. Later DLCCIW follows up on the cases.

- *Legal aid counseling*

Legal services are provided to the victims who are interested to file complaints against abusers. The committee is formed with lawyers, social workers, doctors. Therefore providing services to the victims does not follow a much longer process.

5.10.1.3 SwadharGreh Home, Woodwichee

The following processes are followed for dealing with the cases in SwadharGreh, Woodwichee:

- *Emergency Rescue and Response*

1. The organization goes for rescue if they get information about any incidence.
2. Sometimes the Panchayat informs them with details about the violence.

3. On getting the information a team from the organization visits the house of the victim.
4. Through a home visit, an effort is made to understand the situation and initiate a preliminary talk with the victim.
5. If the victim shows interest, she is brought to the shelter home otherwise stays with family.
6. After coming to SwadharGreh the victim fills up a registration form containing socio-demographic information with the nature of violence.
7. After having a proper analysis of the given information, the victim is asked about her choice for life. As per her wish, the next step of work is planned.

- *Medical Facility*

1. The inmates are taken to Medical College or civil hospital in case of any health issues immediately after registering their cases.
2. Sometimes the organization organizes a health check-up camp in the home itself.
3. They have empanelled doctors who make visits to the organization every month for health check-up purposes.
4. The inmates are provided with free medicines.

- *Counseling*

1. In house counseling session is done with the inmates to improve their psycho-social condition.
2. If required their family members are called for attending counseling sessions

- *Legal Services*

The organization does not provide legal assistance directly to the inmates but if an inmate wants to take legal advice then they are made connected with District Legal Services Authority.

- *Vocational Training*

1. The inmates are provided with vocational training. The organisation has a tailoring training program and a bamboo & Cane training programme.
2. Depending upon the interest and skill of the inmates, training is facilitated to them.

- *Shelter*

1. The organization provides shelter to the women who approach them directly and indirectly referred by other organizations

2. The shelter is offered for lifelong free of cost.
3. Shelter home provides working opportunities to women. They can work outside and earn their livelihood.

5.11 Problems faced by the Organisation

To some extent all three select organizations are facing some kind of problems while delivering their services to the target population. During interaction with the functionaries such problems have been identified and discussed below in detail:

5.11.1 Problems faced by Sakhi One-Stop Centre

Table 5.27: Problems faced by Sakhi One Stop Centre

Category	Problems faced by the support providing agencies in delivering their services	Major Problems Identified
Emergency Response and Rescue Service	One-Stop Centre (OSC) is open for providing services 24x7. Therefore, the staffs of the organization share their duty in shifts. But because of the shortage of staff in the office sometimes it may not become possible to attend emergency cases at midnight and thus the victims remain deprived of receiving rescue services under OSC.	Understaffed
	Many a time it happened after approaching police in case of emergency rescue, the center has not received any support from the police which further made the center known for the failure of saving people in an emergency.	Lack of cooperation
	There is no dedicated fund to safeguard and focus on causalities throughout an extended time frame in OSC.	Financial Constraint
	There is no dedicated fund for testing and examining victims to provide medical aid.	No dedicate fund
	Victims do not always agree to be examined and tested for medical aid.	Convincing victim for clinical guide

	The Government hospitals like Silchar Medical College & Hospital/ Civil hospital have the proper procedure of giving treatment and abide by such procedure is mandatory for all patients which sometimes require time. Bearing this becomes difficult for the victims and starts creating a chaotic situation in the hospital itself. Though empanelled doctor is there in the centre for consultation but for conducting different examinations and tests government hospitals are preferred since they offer services free of cost.	Managing victims' behavior in public
Assistance to women in lodging FIR/ NCR/DIR	When the victims seek assistance from the Centre in lodging FIR against the abuser, it always does not become possible to accompany them to the police station because of work pressure and limited staff which later turns out to be a factor of criticism and dissatisfaction on the part of victims.	Limited staff
	The centre connects the victim with the police stations but after going there victims are not well heard and their cases are not made registered. If they respond even then it takes time to lodge the FIR.	Questionable service providing system
	The entire process compels the victim to re-think about filing FIR and it happened in many cases that after going police station the victims returned without filing the case and blamed the center for being non-cooperative towards the vulnerable.	Work pressure
	Sometimes victims refuse to attend to the police station and file FIR because they are concerned about society's stigma and their family's image. In some cases thinking of refusal from the husband's side restricts women to file a case against abusers.	The non-cooperative attitude of the police Being blamed for non-cooperation. Counselling to victims for taking the right decisions
	Sometimes victims do not uncover current realities about the occurrence, rather shares a misleading case situation, and finding out the real facts consumes time, energy, and resources.	Not serious about counselling sessions

	It happened in some cases when functionaries of the centre could not reach the victims during home-based counselling or follow-up sessions due to the false address given by the victim.	Mental preparedness for counselling
	In some cases, the service providers could not identify the victim's home and if they find out, the residence is found either locked or if it is not locked, people did not respond positively. As a result, the cases had been onthe pending list for quite some time and reopening the case becomes difficult if any of them approach to do so.	Faulty information causes a delay in the problem-solving process
	The centre fails to provide timely support services to the victims because of this incorrect information. Victims do not always pay attention during psychosocial support and counselling sessions.	Unable toprovide timely support services
Legal aid and counseling	For providing free legal help services, victims are made connected with the District Legal services authority (DLSA). It happened in many situations when the victims did not get a proper response from the lawyers and on behalf of the centre also could not extend much support in this regard. Lawyers were committed to other cases and thus convincing them for the new cases was a challenge for the centre.	Time taking process
	The victimsrefused to seek legal aid counselling in some circumstances due to social stigma and family reputation.	Convincing lawyers
	Many victims believe that if they seek legal assistance, their husbands/in-laws will refuse to accept them back into their homes.	Combating fear of victim about non-acceptance by the husband, family, and society.
Shelter	The emergency shelter facility was provided to the victims for 2/3 days. After that, if they require shelter, they are made shifted to other shelter homes. In such a situation the victims do not like to relocate and forcing them to leave OSC becomes a daunting task.	Lack of seat capacity
	In other circumstances, the victims do not want to stay in the shelter home and apply many unfair means to go out of the shelter home. Complaining about not getting basic amenities is a regular phenomenon.	Use of unfair means to get out of the shelter home

5.11.2 Problems faced by District Level Committee for Crime Involving Women (DLCCIW)

Table 5.28: Problems faced by DLCCIW

Category	The problems faced by the support providing agencies in delivering their services	Major Problems Identified
Emergency Response and Rescue Service	Victims do not want to register the case with registration fees and try to get it registered using other means which creates a problem for the office-bearers.	Not interested in paying Case registration fees and using unfair means for registration defaming organization's reputations
	On receiving the notice by the offender party they visit the office of DLCCIW but many are there who neither appear before the committee nor inform anything to the committee which not only makes the entire process of seeking justice delayed but also hampers the women psychologically.	Non-adherence of the notice by the offenders
Psycho-social support/ counseling	The victim doesn't pay much importance to the counselling session though they expressed it helps them immensely.	Generating awareness about the importance of counselling
	Sometimes because of the infringed restrictions on movement by the husband, the victim can't come out from home for attending sessions.	Convincing family members for attending counselling sessions
	The offender party shows irregularity in attending counselling sessions and the case remains on the pending list and the victims are to bear with the abusive relationship.	To make the offender party regular for counselling sessions
	Bringing two parties together for the session becomes challenging for the agency personnel.	Taking two parties in confidence for resolving the problem
Legal aid and counseling	Both parties should attend a legal aid counselling session, however occasionally the second party/ offender does not turn up and the counselling session goes in vain	Motivating the second party for attending counseling session
	On occasions when legal procedures take time the offender's party creates nuisance in the court campus and humiliates the victim in front of all. Such behaviour not only spoils the work environment but also affects the dignity of the women.	Misbehavior on the part of second party in the court campus

5.11.3 Problems faced by SwadharGreh (Woodwichee)

Table 5.29: Problems faced by SwadharGreh

Category	The problems faced by the support providing agencies in delivering their services	Major problems identified
Emergency Response and Rescue Service	The rescue team of the organization does not have police personnel which sometimes challenge the rescue team to conduct rescue operation smoothly.	No police personnel in the rescue team
	At the time of home visits many a time, it happened that victims are denied filing any such cases to the organization.	Non-acceptance of the cases being filed by the victim
Medical Assistance	Sometimes victims deny medical check-ups and convincing them for a check-up is a difficult job. Even if they agree they would put forward their choices. If it is Government hospitals like Medical college then they would agree to go and if it is a Primary health centre they create a problem. But sometimes to avoid the crowd organization prefers to take the victim to Primary health centres.	Conducting medical examinations
	There were cases when young unmarried victims became pregnant and were not sharing accurate information about their pregnancy but had new stories every day. They were not even ready to consult doctors arranged by the organization. In such a situation taking them to other doctors and controlling their aggressive behaviour becomes a little problematic for the organization.	Misleading the organisation with false information
Psycho-social support/ counseling	Since the inmates get the opportunity to work outside the shelter home so they behave like they know everything, the social scene is not unknown to them so counselling is not required for them.	Making them motivated for attending counseling sessions
	Victims occasionally disclose fake experiences, therefore sometimes organizations fail to work out and solve problems through counselling.	Fake information debars the organizations to provide the best services

Legal aid and counseling	The District Legal Service Authority (DLSA) is obliged to give legal aid and counselling to victims, but in practice, victims do not always receive legal assistance.	Inadequate legal help is provided by DLSA
	Obtaining assistance takes a long time and requires a complicated procedure; hence victims were unable to obtain these services.	Lengthy legal procedures
Shelter	Conflict among the inmates is a daily episode and managing conflict is even more difficult.	Limited seat capacity in the shelter home
	Restriction on movement and following of strict timetable is not liked by the victim and thus they sometimes create a chaotic situation.	Disciplined life
	Though everything is provided to them yet sometimes they make complain about not providing quality food.	Complain about basic amenities

5.12 Approaches adopted as a response strategy to the problems

Relationship building: Taking initiatives for creating positiverelationships with the police and inviting them to grace any programme organized by them is one such initiative. According to the functionaries, such an approach is yielding beneficial results.

Coordination: The functionaries are coordinating with the staff for shifting duty so that emergency support services can be provided to all who approach the support organizations. The organizations are also coordinating with other organizations with whom they are working in collaboration.

Rapport building with the clients: The organizations are emphasising more on building rapport with the clients. They are working on developing reciprocal trust, companionship, and empathy with someone. Trying to make the victim feel comfortable and assuring them that confidentiality will be maintained about their cases.

Counseling: The organizations are focusing more on improving counseling skills so that they can assist and guide the victim professionally to resolve their problems especially interpersonal, social, and psychological problems and difficulties. They are trying to resolve client's concerns positively by assisting the client with explaining their issues, exploring options, and fostering approaches to enhance self-consciousness.

Collaboration: The organizations have collaborated with the department of social work, Assam University, Silchar, and with other Non-Government Organizations to:

a) Organise awareness programmes on domestic violence issues
b) Generate awareness about the services of support providing agencies
c) Facilitate the victims with legal assistance
d) Provide psycho-social counselling to the victims
e) Make impact analysis of the counselling sessions

5.13 Suggestions for improving service delivery

The organizations were asked to share ways to improve service delivery. The responses of all three organizations are taken together and mentioned below:

- Domestic abuse cases are particularly delicate and must be handled professionally with skills and approaches. The personnel tasked with dealing with domestic violence may be highly skilled. As a result, continuous training and follow-up of employees' activities in service are important.
- There is a requirement for sufficient staff in addition to qualified staff. All the select organizations expressed dissatisfaction with their staffing pattern. Domestic abuse crimes frequently necessitate one-on-one therapy, requiring dedicated staff to handle each case, which demands increasing manpower or employing appropriate manpower proportionate to the instances.
- Funding is also required for organizations to operate and provide services efficiently. Due to a lack of funds, organizations are to compromise with certain important components like awareness generation and home visits to reach vulnerable women. According to the functionaries, Government may make stringent plans in this regard and organizations may also develop an effective fund-raising plan among potential donors.
- Counseling sessions are at the centre of such an organization's offerings. However, ignoring the sessions or failing to show attention has an impact on the counseling programmes' effectiveness. Such programmes should be strengthened, and proper counseling improves the position of both parties involved in many cases. Proper counseling will encourage family members to attend sessions, and the parties' regularities will be enhanced, reducing the time it takes to resolve the issue. Therefore, it was suggested to increase awareness about the importance of counseling in problem-solving.
- Victims frequently withhold factual information which obstructs the smooth delivery of services. Faulty information also slows down the problem-solving process. Thus, accurate data must be obtained and facts carefully validated.

- The victims frequently express apprehension about being alone and abandoned by their husbands and relatives. This dread must be combated with effective therapy, and they may be assisted in fighting for their rights and escaping the precarious situation induced by domestic violence.
- The seat capacity and the duration of stay in the shelter home may be increased.
- There is a need to improve police cooperation. The police must accompany the rescue crew and provide full help in filing a police report and performing other actions. If police coordination is improved, issues such as non-payment of case registration fees, using unfair ways to obtain shelter housing, or offenders failing to comply with the notice would be addressed.
- The Panchayat, Muslim clergy, and other local officials should be invited to accompany the victims in the early phases of the investigation. This will help to start a healthy discussion and will also help to verify facts.
- The office must have a dedicated health worker assigned to it who will correctly commence health components such as medical examinations, rescue and relief, health checks, and the resolution of any medical difficulties resulting from the violence.
- Legal process must be adequate and timely.
- To generate either a job of opportunity or adequate training to enable one to become economically self-reliant. So that women who have been victims of domestic abuse and have been left to suffer can live a better life.
- Service providers as a whole is not dealing with maintenance issue thus unable to assist the beneficiaries in this regard to which they are legally entitled. As a result, organisations that aid victims of domestic violence may help the women by supporting her in obtaining the correct amount for maintenance.
- Victims of domestic violence frequently feel helpless while dealing with the police. As a result, a lot of time is consumed and resources to complete the case. The service providing organisations can play a facilitator role by assisting victims of domestic violence in filing police complaints and receiving other necessary support.
- It has been discovered that Muslim women victims take years to rebuild or admit to professionals or organizations about the violence perpetrated against them by their husbands and in-laws. Therefore, research should be undertaken in this regard to determine the causes of the problem and the intervention plan to solve the difficulties.

The study was successful in ensuring academic inputs from time to time from different experts. It was among the suggestions given by the experts to understand husbands (males) experience with domestic violence. Therefore, the researcher has done four case studies. The cases were selected from among the select organizations.

5.14 Case study

- ✓ A 24-year young man in Cachar district Mr. Hasan married a girl of 19 years in 2018. They married with the consent of their family members. Mr. Hasanbelonged to a joint family with 26 family members. He was a businessman by profession whose monthly income was approximately Rs. 17000/-. According to him, from the very first day of the marriage, his wife had some adjustment issues with the family members. She was finding it difficult to live comfortably with all the family members despite knowing the family structure before marriage, Hassan said. Therefore, her behavior towards other family members was not so pleasant. However, days were passing and she conceived a baby and preferred to stay separately with her husband. Both Hasan and Rafiya were allowed to stay in a rented house by her in-laws. Since then neither she has taken care of herself nor her husband and developed other health issues. She used to react negatively if any family members enquire about her health and their marital relationship, according to Hasan. The situation was getting worsen and in that condition, only Rafiya has given birth to a boy child. Her health condition didn't permit her to take the best care of herself and her baby yet she was not interested to call anybody from the family for help. Such behavior has impacted their relationships badly. Seeing the mental state of condition of Rafiya, her husband Hasan consulted with doctors and ultimately she has been diagnosed with bipolar disorder and depression. She has undergone different treatment procedures but could not bring much improvement. Hasan has shared the matter with his in-laws. But they were not ready to accept that Rafiya is going through manic episodes. They stated she's perfectly normal. When Hasan disclosed Rafiya's manic episodes, his parents refused to get her back home and wanted Hasan to give divorce his wife. However, Hasan did not give his consent for divorce and thereby staying with his wife and bearing an abusive relationship at home. To minimize the abuse, he approached one of the select organizations seeking counseling. Now both the couples are attending counselling sessions.
- ✓ Mr. Jahir is a 30 years old man married to a woman 25 years old in 2015. It was a love marriage with family consent. The girl was interested in pursuing higher education and thus she was given assurance before marriage for the continuation of her education after marriage and therefore she could complete B. Ed course and eventually qualified for the Assam TET. She has been posted in a school situated in the southern part of the Cachar District. Her parent also resides in the nearby area. The distance between her husband's house to school is approximately 32 km. Mr. Jahir was a Medical Representative by profession. He was drawing a handsome salary every month so he could afford a vehicle to make his wife's journey comfortable. After traveling for a

month, his wife decided to stay with her parents and insisted Jahirtoo stay with her in her parents' house. Jahir did not accept her request and refused to live with her. They lived separately for long two years. During the pendency of two years, Jahir several times went to his wife and tried to convince her to family planning. She denied coming back with him and making plans for a family extension, according to Jahir. He further expressed that he is suspecting his wife of having an extramarital affair and so shows a negative attitude. Such a disturbing relationship continued for long four years and finally, she decided to give him a divorce. She has filed a complaint against him demanding Rs. 30 lakhs as maintenance for abusing her. Their case is under process in the district court.

- ✓ 22 years of age Maksud married Sippon, a 19-year-old, in 2015. It was a love marriage between two people who liked each other but didn't have the support of their families. Maksud's educational qualifications were HSLC, while his wife Sippon's were eight standards. They came from a lower-middle-class background. Maksud's father was an M.E. School teacher at the time of his marriage, and he was unemployed. He gave up his studies after their marriage and began driving. They had two daughters in their marriage. His wife was not a well-mannered woman and did keep the house dirty and unclean. Her husband was often suspected of extramarital affairs, and they fought constantly. If her spouse showed physical advancement, she retaliated by physically abusing him. She did not watch after, care for, or respect her In-laws. Their children were suffering greatly as a result of their dysfunctional relationship. Their daughter avoided social situations. Their daughter didn't discuss anything with anyone and was psychologically unstable. They did not want to stay in this unhealthy relationship. Maksud decided to end this relationship by giving his wife a divorce decree. His wife, however, was not on board with this decision.
- ✓ Lutfur and Forida married in 2017 with the consent of both parties' family members. Forida belonged to the general caste and Lutfur from MOBC. He was employed as a Multi-Purpose Health Worker in the Department of Health (MPW). His family lives in a rural area with other family members and he is the sole earner of the family. He has to care for his elderly parents. His wife never wanted to live in the village and thus she used to insist her husband take her to the city. Lutfur tried to persuade her that he would take her to the city once his younger brother gets married. She, on the other hand, did not agree with it and started behaving differently. She used to wake up late, was not following any religious activity, and was not taking proper care of her in-laws. She always had an attitude of showing her class that she belongs, according to Lutfur, which eventually invited a lot of problems in their marital relationships. In some cases, both had physical violence against the family. She gradually moved to her parent's

house and filed a complaint against Lutfur in court. The case has been going on for the past two years and now both parties want to settle the matter. Fordia demanded Mohor be given to her. Lutfur granted Mohor to her and has taken divorce in Kaji court.

The case studies reflected that adjustment issues, interference of parents, high ambition, extramarital affair, aggressive behavior of women are the causes making the marital relationships abusive and thus disturbed. Generally, we assume that poor financial condition might be a reason for violence at home but in these cases, it was nowhere connected with the aroused problems. Rather joint family structure has been one of the reasons for increasing the cases of violence at home. Different couples have undergone counseling sessions to resolve their problems while others preferred to give a divorce. From the broader perspective, the case studies have reflected that domestic violence issues need a holistic approach to understand and address.

Chapter - 6

Concluding Discussion

Domestic violence among Muslim women has become a threatening matter in the Cachar District of Assam. It was found in the study that numerous factors like health, economic, emotional, sexual, and religious are the factors responsible for domestic violence among Muslim Women in Cachar. Such factors have been leading to physical and emotional violence and affecting a Muslim woman's family relations, social relations, sexual life, children's well-being, and mental health. Different socio-legal support providing agencies like police, court, social organizations have been relentlessly trying to address domestic violence issues in the district through different support services.

Muslim scholars of the past and the present view all forms of domestic violence as forms of oppression and the Quaran and the Hadith are explicit in their prohibition against all forms of oppression, and injustice as clearly stated in the Holy Quran (Abdalla 2004).It indicates that Islam's attitude towards treating women is clear. The Prophet also taught that a Muslim's good character will be reflected through his/her faith and in how he treats his wife.However, as time has changed, the Quran's words have been misconstrued, and males have defied the duties of women, seeing them as inferior and abusing and demeaning them mentally and physically.

The study highlighted that the women hide the evidence of abuse and don't report it to the authorities in Muslim majority communities. Therefore, the prevalence of the problem remains unknown; despite Muslim feminists' belief that it is widespread. Various ideas about violence against women have been discussed, including Feminist Theory, Socio-Psychological Theories, Frustration-Aggression Theory, Patriarchal Theory, and so on. Multiple theories have added new dimensions to our understanding of domestic violence. According to feminist ideology, gender inequality and oppression victimize the female population. According to socio-psychological theory, offenders' psychological disorders lead to aggressiveness against women.

It is found in the study that the majority of the Muslim victims were married when they were 16-20 years old and experienced domestic violence right away, and reported their abuse by the time they were 23-27 years old. The bulk of Muslim marriages that culminate in domestic violence according to the report, are arranged by family members, and the women begin their lives with strangers, are abused, and eventually divorce. The study has also reported that most of the cases of domestic violence were from joint families. Moreover, the victims had only minimal education and the majority of them were homemakers with zero income, limiting their economic independence and making their lives more vulnerable. It is understood from the study that Domestic violence against Muslim women in Assam's Cachar district was caused by a variety of factors that led to violence.

The study presented that approximately 82.03 percent became victims of domestic abuse because of health reasons. Economic variables accounted for 51.56 percent of the respondents; sexual elements accounted for 78.13 percent; religious factors accounted for 91.41 percent; and emotional factors accounted for 100 percent of the respondents. According to the data, adverse health concerns & stress and worry of husbands cause tension, mood swings, and a chaotic situation at home. There are also some instances of chronic health difficulties contributing to domestic violence. Economic issues were also indicated as a contributing factor to violence which has affected the victims in all aspects.

Mental torture, neglect, and physical beating were the most common forms of violence. According to the research, the most common kind of abuse is being humiliated for no apparent reason followed by being mistreated for sharing their opinions on family or financial matters. There are also cases when victims are nagged regularly on minor issues. The mode of physical violence was diverse in nature. The victims were subjected to arm twisting & slapping, hurling with objects, and being kicked and dragged out of the home. Their self-esteem had been devastated by such physical assault, and they were living a life devoid of dignity. Muslim women under consideration have diminished their sexual feelings for their husbands and they feel disgusted with their husband's sexual advancement. Sex under compulsion was another factor affected the sexual relations of women. According to the study, the husbands' sexual wants and demands are more important than the personal preferences of the wives, and victims must comply with their wishes even if they are uninterested. The episode of violence at home has not only affected the women but also badly affected the children as well.

In accordance with the findings, Husbands were the primary perpetrators of domestic abuse, followed by their in-laws. The vast majority of those respondents had been victims of domestic violence for more than five years. The respondents believed that their husbands are misled by the belief that men are superior to women and, as a result, always act in an authoritarian manner and also that their husbands blindly accept religious leaders' instructions, restricting women from being exposed to modernity, etc., is pushing women deeper into vulnerability.

Even if they want to react to the circumstance, they couldn't, thinking about the future of their children. Finding no other option they choose to scream and cry immediately after the violence to outburst their anger & frustration. Domestic violence has shattered the peace of the family and put conjugal relations under pressure. Muslim women in Cachar who are victims of domestic abuse have yet to speak out or fight for their rights, instead of choosing silence.

To come out of this difficult situation the sufferer initially has to approach their in-laws and parents for proper guidance and support. Surprisingly, 91.40 percent of Muslim women have not received any support from their in-laws and In contrast, 94.53 percent of women received guidance from their parents. Women were suggested by their parents to consult with socio-legal support providing agencies working on domestic violence or to give another chance to their relationship. Choosing the latter, the respondents have approached many organizations like the police department, family court, Panchayat, district court, district social welfare department, and social organizations to register their cases. Of which Panchayat has recorded the highest number of cases as reported by the study. It is understood that Panchayat plays a crucial role in assisting Muslim women victims of domestic violence.

The victims usually look for different services from the approached organizations and departments like shelter, family counseling, rescue, and legal assistance. The majority of respondents were dissatisfied with the intervention made by the approached organization, and some said the organizations could only partially solve their difficulties. This led to the respondents being ready to approach organizations exclusively working on domestic violence issues and offering services as per the need of the victim in the Cachar district of Assam.

Subsequently, they have approached organizations like One-stop center, DLCCIW &SwadharGreh were providing different services like: I) Legal aid counseling, ii) Psycho-social counseling, iii) Medical assistance, iv) Assistance in lodging FIR/NCR/DIR,v) Rescue & response vi) Emergency shelter,vii) Legal services, viii) Vocational training. Initially, they were not aware of these organizations but later on, they have come to know about these organizations from different sources like parents & family members, Government officials, Friends, newspapers, and local clubs.Besides domestic violence cases, organizations like one-stop centers focus on human trafficking and kidnapping, DLCCIW focuses on property-related concerns, and SwadharGreh emphasizes giving shelter to domestic abuse victims. The process of dealing with cases is almost similar to all the select organizations. The complaints are received either directly or through the 181 toll-free number. On receiving the complaint, the process starts as per the agency's set procedures.

The process of dealing with cases is almost similar to all the select organizations. The complaints are received either directly or through the 181 toll-free number. On receiving complaints, the process starts as per the agency's set guidelines. The services provided on different components like could solve the problems partially for the majority of the victims. The women whose problems remained unsolved have preferred to stay with their husbands compromising on the situation and some preferred to stay with their parents when some are striving for ensuring economic stability. Among the many, the psycho-social counseling service has greatly benefited the victims. The majority of the women have expressed their satisfaction in terms of receiving the services while a negligible number have shown dissatisfaction with components like vocational training, rescue, etc.

In their opinion, vocational training could have been provided for a longer duration to create an impact on the economic development of the victims. Adding to that they said many a time it had happened that even after informing the concerned organization they have not come to the rescue. When the matter was enquired with the organization it has come to the notice that supports providing agencies were facing many challenges and problems with regards to i) staff, ii) funds, iii) cooperation, iv) managing victim's behavior, v) fake supply of information, vi) low self-esteem of victims, vi) seat capacity in a shelter home, vii) unfair means to leave shelter home, viii) non-adherence of office order, ix) payment of registration fees, x) generating awareness, xi) convincing for family counseling.

According to them, running the center with limited staff is a challenging task and finance is one of the major problems which give birth to other problems. In their opinion, financial constraint debars them from organizing awareness camps on issues of importance and destroys the work spirit of the employees as they are not given their salaries timely. It is because of shortage of funds, inmates are made deprived of many services which as per guidelines should be provided with and thus becomes a reason of dissatisfaction for the victims.

During interaction with the functionaries, the investigator came to know that sometimes they fail to ensure cooperation from police and legal advisors which make the entire process of service delivery delayed. Sometimes, the aggressive behavior of the parties on the court campus or the premises of other organizations not only hampers the work culture but also puts the victim's image in crisis and such behavior becomes difficult on some occasions. According to the functionaries, the faulty information provided by the victims not only misleads the professionals but also affects the smooth process of dealing with the cases, and responding to victims' problems immediately does not always become possible.

Even if they are asked to attend counseling sessions, they don't turn up but the victims expressed that counseling helps them most. Preparing them mentally for attending counseling sessions was again a challenge for the organizations. It was understood from the study that victims were inclined to legal aid consultations from district legal services authority to improve their lives along with their kids by reducing the recurring incidences of domestic violence. However, getting time from the lawyers was a challenge for the victims and they used to blame the organizations for not extending support in this regard.

It was expressed by one of the organisation that registration fees are the source of generating fund which is needed to run the organisation. But the complainants often use unfair means to avoid paying registration fees, affecting the reputation of the organisation. Many inmates staying in the shelter home expressed that seat capacity has to be increased and the functionaries too believe the same as victim's demands to stay in a shelter home for more than five days in some cases. When victims demand shelter and organizations fail to provide it, the victim party creates a chaotic situation. There are also cases when inmates use unfair means to go out of the shelter home and later it becomes a problem in tracing them. Moreover, some organizations don't have police personnel in the rescue team which altogether makes the rescue process more critical.

The support-providing agencies have adopted different approaches to making the service delivery system smooth amidst problems and challenges. The approaches are i) relationship building, ii) coordination, iii) rapport building with the clients, iv) counselling, v) collaboration.

Muslim women are trapped in violent relationships for a variety of reasons. Despite being in an abusive relationship, Muslim women prefer to live with the abusers because of their financial insecurities, parents' reputations, kids' future, and having no alternative place to stay. Surprisingly all the 128 respondents (100 percent) felt that domestic violence affected family relations in general and couple relations in particular. The victims also got socially aloof as they felt embarrassed to face their neighbors. Because of the screams and assaults at home, they were even terrified to show their faces. The study found that the victims were under mental stress and had sleep difficulty.

Quran allows polygamy marriage but it is restricted to a maximum of four wives with a condition to treat all wives equally in terms of love, care, and respect. Islam viewed women as a mother, a wife, a helper and a supporter. Even though the Quran emphasizes equality, there is a huge disparity in status enjoyed by men and women particularly in villages (Al-Mannai). Islam does not encourage divorce but most Muslim scholars view divorce as a better option for those who are not happy in their matrimonial relationship and their relationship has broken down because of any reason.

Islam prefers the reunion of two conflicting parties and canceling divorce during the reconciliation time. It allows divorce only when it is understood that living together in harmony for both the couples would be impossible and all sorts of efforts made to bring peace in the relationship could not yield any positive result. The study also reflected that majority of the women are trying their best to improve the family situation by mutual discussion staying with the husband.

The study has also recorded the voice of Muslim women victims in the form of suggestions like i) mass awareness generation on issues of domestic violence, ii) awareness generation about the services provided by the support providing agencies, iii) strict enforcement of laws, etc. The functionaries of different organizations have also suggested measures for smooth service delivery of services like the timely release of funds for massive awareness drive at the community level and keeping employees of the organization motivated for community work.

However, the study based on the data reported that Muslim women in Cachar had equivalent or even better circumstances than Hindu women. In the Cachar district, Hindus were more likely than Muslims to be victims of domestic abuse.

The interaction with the Muslim women victims along with their family members, chief functionaries of the organizations, and from the personal experience of the researcher it can be said that the nature of domestic violence is almost similar to all women across the country. In some cases, unique factors based on faith, belief, and practices play an important role in violence at home. The person concerned, the government, and support providing agencies from their end have been trying their best to improve the condition. It would not be possible for each stakeholder to fight the situation alone and bring peace, freedom, and security. It requires a collaborative approach, people's active participation, as well as active social groups which can help to alleviate the problem of domestic violence in Cachar.

To have a better understanding of the male perspective, the researchers conducted some case studies. It has been shown that, while domestic violence against women is widespread, there are also instances where women play the victim card. When men perceive injustice being done to their family members, they become enraged, this is misinterpreted as violence against women. When a woman's requests are not granted, she accuses her husband and in-laws of mistreating her. There are numerous examples of this. However, because the study is primarily focused on violence against Muslim women, the male perspective has been underemphasized, and the study has only focused on female victims. However, this leaves the door open for further research into the males who fall victim to this unfortunate predicament.

The study has given some suggestions for the prevention and protection of Muslim women from domestic violence. The suggestions were mainly enhancing education, ensuring economic freedom, improved socialization, correct age at marriage, safeguarding human rights, equality in gender roles, objecting dowry, getting to know the spouse, awareness generation, capacity building, increasing the shelter homes, introducing of helplines, early case proceedings, community sensitization programs, rural services, and strict monitoring.

Diagrammatic Representation – Snapshot of the Study

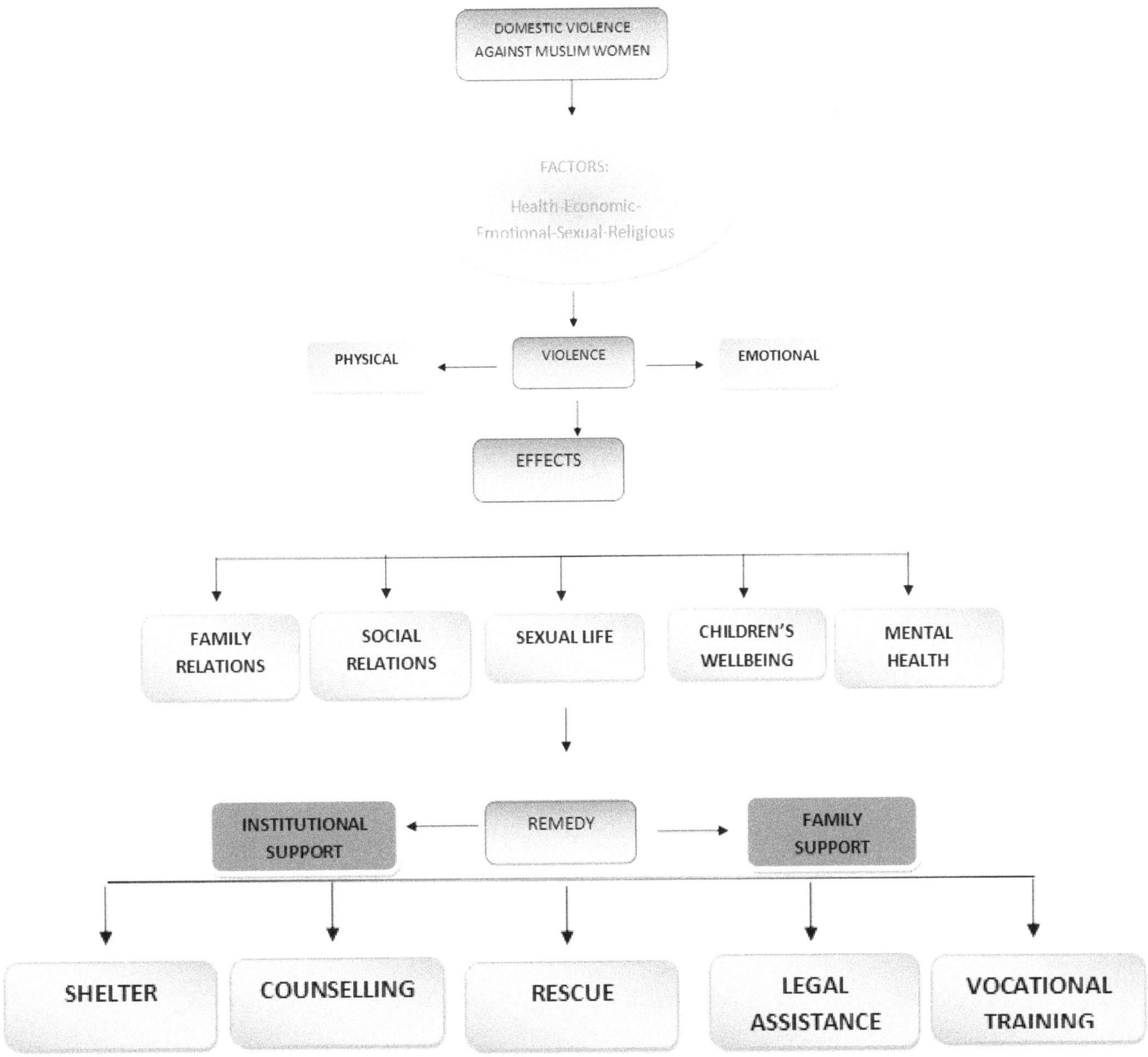

Diagram 6.1: Snapshot of the Study

Bibliography

Afkhami, M., Erturk, Y., & Mayer, A. E. (2019). Feminist advocacy, family law and violence against women: international perspectives. *UK and New York: Routledge, and Ottawa: IDRC.* ISBN 9781138344938, 268. doi:10.1080/13552074.2020.1717196.

Afkhamzadeh, A., Azadi, N.A., Ziaeei, S., & Bolbanabad, A.M. (2019). Domestic violence against women in west of Iran: the prevalence and related factors.*International Journal of Human Rights in Healthcare,* 12(5), 364-372, ISSN 2056-4902. doi:10.1108/IJHRH-12-2018-0080.

Aggarwal, A. (2005). "Feel good" women? Domestic violence perspective. In K. Uma Devi (Eds.). *Violence against women: Human rights perspective,* New Delhi: Serial Publications.

Ahmad, S. M. (2019). Islamophobic violence as a form of gender-based violence: a qualitative study with Muslim women in Canada. *Journal of gender-based violence*, *3*(1), 45-66.

Ahmed, S., & Mistry, M. (2010). Modern Education and Socio-Economic change: A case study of Muslim women in Pune city, India. *Journal of Arts Science & Commerce*, 1(1), 139-149.

Ahuja, R. (1998). Violence against Women. *Rawat Publications, Jaipur and New Delhi*. Retrieved from https://www.rawatbooks.com/women-studies/violence-against-women.

Akgul, F. (2017). Patriarchal Theory Reconsidered: Torture and Gender-Based Violence in Turkey. *Palgrave Macmillan, Cham*, XI, 243, eBook, ISBN 978-3-319-49766-2.

Alharbi, F. F., Alkheraiji, M. A., Aljumah, A. A., Eissa, M. A., Qasim, S. S., & Alaqeel, M. K. (2021). Domestic Violence against Married Women during the COVID-19 Quarantine in Saudi Arabia. *Cureus* 13(5). doi:10.7759/cureus.15231.

Ali, A. (1994). Status of Muslim Women. *Economic & Political Weekly*, 29(6), 297-300.

Aliakbari, S. A., Safarzadeh, S., Bayat, F., Yabandeh, A. P., Dashti, S., Roozbeh, N. & Banaei, M. (2018). Related Factors of Domestic Violence: A Population-Based Research on Iranian Women. *International Journal of Women's Health and Reproduction Sciences,* 6(3), 269–275, ISSN 2330- 4456. doi: 10.15296/ijwhr.2018.45.

Almis, B. H., Kutuk, E. K., Gumustas, F., & Celik, M. (2018). Risk Factors for Domestic Violence i n Women and Predictors of Development of Mental Disorders in These Women. *Arch Neuropsychiatry*, 55, 67−72.doi:org/10.29399/npa.19355.

Ammah, R. (2009). Violence against Women in the Ghanaian Muslim Community in: The Architecture for Violence against Women in Ghana ed. Kathy Cusack and Takyiwaa Manu. Retrieved from http://197.255.68.203/handle/123456789/1732.

An Analysis of Perceptions of Domestic Violence and Efficacy of the Implementation of the PWDV Act. (2005). in Bihar. Retrieved from https://www.careindia.org/wp-content/uploads/2017/05/study-report-R2.pdf.

Arik, H. (2019). Speaking of Women? Exploring Violence against Women through Political Discourses: A Case Study of Headscarf Debates in Turkey. *Open Edition Journals*, ISSN 1647-0737. doi:10.4000/eces.1009.

Asian Journal of Psychiatry. (2020). COVID-19 and domestic violence against women. *Asian Journal of Psychiatry* 53. doi:org/10.1016/j.ajp.2020.102227.

Babu, B., & Kar, S. K. (2009). Domestic violence against women in Eastern India: A population-based study on prevalence and related issues.*BMC Public Health*, 9(1), 129. doi:10.1186/1471-2458-9-129.

Baerveldt, C. (2015). The veil and the search for the self: From identity politics to cultural expression. *Culture & Psychology,* 21(4), 532–545.doi: 10.1177/1354067X15606861.

Banashree, B. (2015). Domestic Violence against Women in Tinsukia District of Assam, India. *Research Journal of Family, Community and Consumer Sciences,*3(4), 1-4.

Bano, S. (1989). Violence on Women in Muslim Society: The case of divorced women. In Niroj Sinha (Eds.). Women and Violence. *New Delhi: Vikash Publishing House.*

Baobaid, M. (2002). Access to Women Abuse Services by Arab-Speaking Muslim Women in London, Ontario. Background Investigation and Recommendations for Further Research and Community Outreach. Centre for Research on Violence against Women and Children, 1-27. Retrieved fromwww.CRVAWC.ca.

Begum, A. R. F. (2014). The Sri Lankan Muslim women's domestic violence: A study based on Koralipattru west Divisional Secretariat Area. *First International Symposium FIA, SEUSL,* 1-45.Retrieved from https://www.seu.ac.lk/researchandpublications/symposium_fia/2014/Islamic%20Thoughts%20Civi/The%20Sri%20Lankan%20Muslim%20womens.pdf.

Bibliography

Bergen, R. K., Edleson, J. L., & Renzetti, C. M. (2011). Source book on VIOLENCE AGAINST WOMEN Second Edition. *Sage Publications, United States of America*, 419, NCJ Number 238123.

Bhattacharya, S., & Bhattacharya, S. (2005). Battered and shattered: will they get justice? A study of domestic violence against women in India based on National Family Health Survey. *The Journal of Adult Protectio,* 244-258, ISSN 1466-8203. doi: 10.1108/JAP-07-2013-0032.

Bhatti, N., Jamali, M. B., Phulpoto, N. N., Mehmood, T., & Shaikh, F.M. (2011). Domestic Violence against Women: A Case Study of District Jacobabad, Sindh Pakistan. *Assian Social Science,* 7(12). doi:10.5539/ass.v7n12p146.

Binswanger, R. (2017). Reconsidering Perversion – a Conceptual Proposal. *Journal für Psychoanalyse*, 57. doi:org/10.18754/jfp.57supp.1.

Borthakur, R. (2016). Violence against Women "With Ecialreference to North East India": Constitutional Provision. *IOSR Journal of Humanities and Social Science (IOSR-JHSS*), 21(10), 54-56, e-ISSN 2279-0837, p-ISSN 2279-0845. doi:10.9790/0837-2110035456.

Cachar District Population Census. (2011). Retrieved from http:/ /www.census 2011.co.in/census/district/144-cachar.html.

Carolin, S. P. A., & Xavier, A.G. (2020). Impact of domestic violence on children: causes and preventive measures. Educere BCM Journal of Social Work (BSW), 16(1).

Chantler, K., Gangoli, G., & Thiara, R. K. (2019). Muslim women and gender based violence in India and the UK. *Critical social policy*, 39(2), 163-183. doi:org/10.1177/0261018318769814.

Choudhary, R., Kaithwas, M., & Rana, G. (2006). Domestic Violence against Women's in India A Study. *PANACEA, International Research Journal,* 1(2),ISSN 2347-369X.

Chowdhury, M. A. K. (2015). Domestic Violence against Women: A Historic and Socio-Cultural Reality in Bangladesh. *European Scientific Journal*, 11(26), 11, ISSN 1857 – 7881.

Cook, K. S., Cheshire, C., Rice, E. R., & Nakagawa, S. (2013). Social exchange theory. *Handbook of social psychology*, 61-88. doi:10.1007/978-94-007-6772-0_3.

Council of Europe. (2010). The Life Cycle and Violence. Retrieved from https://www.endvawnow.org/en/articles/298-the-life-cycle-and violence.html.

Crime in India. (2016). National Crime Record Bureau, Ministry of Home Affairs. Retrieved from https://ncrb.gov.in/en/crime-india-2016-0.

Dalal, K., & Lindqvist, K. (2012). A national study of the prevalence and correlates of domestic violence among women in India. *Asia Pacific Journal of Public Health*, 24(2), 265-277. doi:10.1177/1010539510384499.

Das, K., & Mohanty, B. (2020). The growing concern around violence against women in India – Where do we stand? International Growth Centre (IGC). Retrieved from https://www.theigc.org/blog/the-growing-concern-around-violence-against-women-in-india-where-do-we-stand/.

Diganth Raj Sehgal. (2020). Rights of Muslim women in India. Retrieved from https://blog.ipleaders.in/rights-muslim-women-india/.

Dissolution of Muslim Marriages Act. (1939). Retrieved from http://chdslsa.gov.in/right_menu/act/pdf/muslim.pdf.

District Level Committee for Crimes Involving Women (DLCCIW), Deputy Commissioner's Court, Silchar, Cachar, Assam. Retrieved from http://standupagainstviolence.org/en_US/assam/#cach.

Dogarawa, A. B. (2009). Marriage and Divorce in Islam. *University Library of Munich, Germany*. Retrieved from https://mpra.ub.uni-muenchen.de/id/eprint/23194.

Dorsch, M. J., Tornblom, K. Y., & Kazemi, A. (2017). A review of resource theories and their implications for understanding consumer behavior. *Journal of the Association for Consumer Research*, 2(1), 5-25. doi:org/10.1086/688860.

Dost, M. K. B., Akram, M.W., & Sharifi, S. (2014). An Overview of Theories of Psychopathology with an Emphasis on Addiction. *Journal of Research and Development,* 2(1), 59-65. Retrieved from https://www.arabianjbmr.com/pdfs/RD_VOL_2_1/5.pdf.

Elisabeth, R., Avni, A., Jhumka, G., & Claudia, G. (2020). Violence against women during covid-19 pandemic restrictions. *BMJ*, 369, ISBN 0959-8138. doi: 10.1136/bmj.m1712.

Esraa, O. (2016). Book Review: Domestic Violence and the Islamic Tradition. Journal of International Women's Studies, 17(1), 220-221. Retrieved from https://vc.bridgew.edu/jiws/vol17/iss1/18.

Gabriel, E. (2015). Domestic Violence and Its Effects on Women. *School of Gandhian Thought and Development Studies Mahatma Gandhi University,* Kottyam-686560 Kerala, India. Retrieved from http://hdl.handle.net/10603/165395.

Gaikwad, V., Madhukumar, S., & Sudeepa, D. (2011). An epidemiological Study of Domestic Violence against Women and its Association with Sexually Transmitted Infections in Bangalore Rural. *Online Journal of Health and Allied Sciences,* 10(3),ISSN 0972-5997.

Gama, A., Pedro, R. A., Carvalho, L.J.M., Duarte, V.G.E.A., Quintas, j., Matias, A., & Dias, S. (2021). Domestic Violence during the COVID-19 Pandemic in Portugal. *Port J Public Health,* 38(1), 32–40. doi:10.1159/000514341.

Garg, P. K. (2014). Muslim Personal Law, Uniform Civil Code and Judicial Activism- A Critical Study. Faculty of Law University of Lucknow, U.P. (INDIA).Retrieved from https://www.barandbench.com/apprentice-lawyer/the-uniform-civil-code-judicial-activism.

Gebrewahd, T.G., Gebremeskel, G.G., & Tadesse B. D. (2020). Intimate partner violence against reproductive age women during COVID-19 pandemic in northern Ethiopia: a community-based cross-sectional study. *Gebrewahd et al. Reproductive Health,* 17, 152. doi:org/10.1186/s12978-020-01002-w.

General Assembly. (1962). Convention on Consent to Marriage, Minimum Age for Marriage and Registration of Marriages. *United Nations Human Rights. Office of the High Commissione.* Retrieved from https://www.ohchr.org/en/instruments-mechanisms/instruments/convention-consent-marriage-minimum-age-marriage.

General Recommendation Violence against women. (1992). *UN Committee on the Elimination of Discrimination against Women (CEDAW).* Retrieved from https://www.refworld.org/docid/52d920c54.html.

Government of India, Census. (2011). *Population by Religious Community*. Retrieved from http://www.censusindia.gov.in/2011census/population _enumeration.html.

Government of India. (2006). National Family Health Survey. Final Report NFHS-III. New Delhi: Ministry of Health and Family Welfare. Retrieved from https://dhsprogram.com/pubs/pdf/frind3/frind3-vol1andvol2.pdf.

Gulati, G., & Kelly, B. D. (2020). Domestic violence against women and the COVID-19 pandemic: What is the role of psychiatry? *Int J Law Psychiatry*, 71, ISBN 101594. doi:10.1016/j.ijlp.2020.101594.

Hajjar, L. (2004). “Religion, State Power, and Domestic Violence in Muslim Societies: A Framework for Comparative Analysis”.*Law and Social Inquiry*, 29(1), 1–38.

Hasan, Z., & Menon, R. (2004). Unequal citizens- A study of Muslim women in India. *New Delhi:Oxford University Press*, ISBN: 019566535X.

Hulya, A. (2012). Speaking of Women? Exploring Violence against Women through Political Discourses: A Study of Headscraf Debates in Turkey. *e-cadernos CES,* 16, 10-31,ISSN 1647-0737. doi:10.4000/eces.1009.

ICRW. (2004). Violence against Women in India: A Review of Patterns, Trends and Responses. *Lodi Estrate-New Delhi, India*. Retrieved from https://india.unfpa.org/sites/default/files/pub-pdf/435.pdf.

Information Series on Sexual and Reproductive Health and Rights, Violence Against Women, *United Nations Human Rights. Office of the High Commissione.* Retrieved from https://www.ohchr.org/Documents/Issues/Women/WRGS/SexualHealth/INFO_VAW_WEB.pdf.

Iregui-Bohórquez, A. M., Ramírez-Giraldo, M. T., & Tribín-Uribe, A. M. (2019). Domestic Violence against Rural Women in Colombia: The Role of Labour Income. *Feminist Economics*. doi:org/10.1080/13545701.2019.1566752.

Isgandarova, N. (2017). The Role of Islam in Preventing Domestic Violence towards Muslim Women in Azerbaijan. *Spiritual Psychology and Counselling,* 183-200, eISSN 2458-9675. doi:10.12738/spc.2017.2.0019.

Islamic Society of North America. (2009). The Islamic Response to Domestic Violence. *Ethnomed*. Retrieved from https://ethnomed.org/resource/the-islamic-response-to-domestic-violence/.

Jackson, N.A. (2007). Encyclopedia of Domestic Violence. *Routledge, New York*. doi:org/10.4324/9780203942215.

Jasrotia, A. (2012). An Empirical Study of Crime against Women: A Study of Union Territory Chandigarh.*Asian Journal of Multidimensional Research,* 1(1), ISSN 2278-4853.

Jawarkar, A.K., Shemar, H., Wasnik, V. R., & Chavan, S. M. (2016).Domestic violence against women: A Cross-Sectional study in rural area of Amravati district of Maharashtra, India. *International Journal of Research in Medical Sciences,* 4(7), ISBN 2713-2718.

Jena, D.K., & Acharya, S.S. (2014). Domestic Violence against Women as a Human Rights Violation: A Study of the District Of Balasore. *International Journal of Social Science and Humanities Research,* 2(4), 350-362, ISSN 2348-3164. Retrieved from www.researchpublish.com.

Johnson, A. J. (2015). Religion and Men's Violence against Women. *Springer, New York, NY*, XXV, 474, ISBN 978-1-4939-2266-6. doi:org/10.1007/978-1-4939-2266-6.

Jones, C. R., & Isham. L. (2020). The pandemic paradox: The consequences of COVID-19 on domestic violence. *John Wiley & Sons Ltd,* 29, ISBN 2047–2049. doi: 10.1111/jocn.15296.

Kalokhe, A., Rio, C. R., C., Dunkle, K., Stephenson, R., Metheny, N., Paranjape, A., &Sahay, S. (2017). Domestic violence against women in India: A systematic review of a decade of quantitative studies. *Glob Public Health*, 12(4), 498–513. doi: 10.1080/17441692.2015.1119293.

Kar, N. B., & Ghosh, B. N. (2017). Education and Socio-economic Marginalization of Muslim Women: A Case Study of North 24-Parganas District in West Bengal. *Bangladesh e-Journal of Sociology.* 14(1), 129-149.

Kar, P.K. (2009). Domestic Violence: Need for Legal Awareness. *Dominant Publisher and Distributors Published by A.S Saini for Dominant Publishers and Distributors,* ISBN 81-7888-683-9,Printed at Orient Offset, Delhi-110053.

Kazi, S. (1999). Muslim Women in India. *Minority Rights Group*, 1-40, ISBN 1897693478.

Khadenga, B. (2009). Domestic Violence and Legal Awareness: The Indian Scenario. *Published by A.S Saini for Dominant Publishers and distributors*, Printed at orient offset, Delhi, ISBN 81-7888-683-9.

Khalid, S. (2013). Violence against Women. *Canadian Council of Muslim Women. Health and Justice for Canadian Muslim Women*, 1-198, ISBN 978-0-9688621-9-3. Retrieved from http://cdhpi.ca/sites/cdhpi.ca/files/VAW_health_Justice.pdf.

Khatri, R. B., & Pandey, B. K. (2013). Causes of violence against women: A qualitative study at Bardiya district. *Health Prospect: Journal of Public Health*, 12(1). doi:org/10.3126/hprospect.v12i1.8721.

Khatun, T., & Rahman, K. F. (2012). Domestic Violence against Women in Bangladesh: Analysis from a Socio-legal Perspective.*Bangladesh e-Journal of Sociology,* 9(2).

Kiruthika. (2013). A Statistical Study on Nature and Extent of Violence against Women in Puducherry. *IOSR Journal of Humanities and Social Science (IOSR-JHSS),* 18(1), 1-5,e-ISSN 2279-0837, p-ISSN 2279-0845.Retrieved from www.iosrjournals.org.

Korte, A.M. (2011). Openings: A Genealogical Introduction to Religion and Gender. *Religion and Gender,* 1, 1-17, ISSN 1878-5417, *Publisher: Igitur Publishing (Utrecht)*. Retrieved from www.religionandgender.org. URN: NBN: NL: UI: 10-1-101587.

Kozieł, P. (2017). Gender-Based Violence in Northern Nigeria. The Context of Muslim and Christian Women's Rights. *Hemispheres*, 32, 41-53, ISBN 978-83-7452-08-4.

Krishnakumar, A., & Verma, S. (2021). Understanding Domestic Violence in India during COVID-19: a Routine Activity Approach. *Asian Journal of Criminology,* 16, 19–35. doi:org/10.1007/s11417-020-09340-1.

Laeheem, K. (2014). Causes of domestic violence between Thai Muslim married couples in Satun province. *Asian Social Science*, 10(21), 89. doi:10.5539/ass.v10n21p89.

Laskar, A. I. (2016). Human Rights and Women A Study Of Violence against Muslim Women in Barak Valley. *Ph.D Thesis, Shodhganga*. Retrieved from http://hdl.handle.net/10603/292521.

Laskar, N. H. (2014). Violence against Women: Female Foeticide and Infanticide. *An Annual Research Journal of Business Studies,* ISSN: 2249-4545.

Lunn, J. (2009). The Role of Religion, Spirituality and Faith in Development: a critical theory approach. Third World Quarterly, 30(5), 937-951. doi:10.1080/01436590902959180.

Lyons, S. D., & Berge, Z. L. (2012). Social Learning Theory. In: Seel N.M. (Eds.). Encyclopedia of the Sciences of Learning. Springer, Boston, MA. doi:org/10.1007/978-1-4419-1428-6_1257.

Maternity Benefit Act. (1961). Retrieved from https://labour.gov.in/sites/default/files/TheMaternityBenefitAct1961.pdf.

Misra, P. (2007). Domestic violence against women. *Deep & Deep Publications Pvt. Ltd.* F-259, Rajouri Garden, New Delhi-110027, ISBN 81-7629-896-4.

Mlambo-Ngcuka, P. (2020). Violence against women and girls: the shadow pandemic, *United Nation Women*. Retrieved from https://www.unwomen.org/en/news/stories/2020/4/statement-ed-phumzile-violence-against-women-during-pandemic.

Mohammedan Law. Sources of Muslim Personal Law. Retrieved from https://www.toppr.com/guides/legalaptitude/family-law-I/mohammedan-law-sources-of-muslim-personal-law/.

Mooney, J. (2000). Gender Violence and the Social Order. Palgrave Macmillan UK, 1, 260-261, ISBN 978-0-333-91886-9. doi:10. 1057/9780230597396.

MWCD. (2015). Working Women Hostel. Retrieved from https://womenandchildren.assam.gov.in/sites/default/files/Working%20Women%20Hostel.pdf.

MWCD. (2017). Pradhan Mantri Matru Vandana Yojana. Retrieved from https://socialwelfare.assam.gov.in/sites/default/files/swf_utility_folder/departments/sw_webcomindia_org_oid_3/menu/document/pmmvy_scheme_implementation_guidelines_-_mwcd_compressed.pdf.

Nanette, D. J. (1988). Shelters for battered women: Social policy response to interpersonal violence. The Social Science Journal,25(4), 401-419. doi: org/10.1016/0362-3319(88)90021-3.

Narain, V. (2013). Muslim women's equality in India: Applying a human rights framework. *Human Rights Quarterly,* 35(1), 91–115, Published By: The Johns Hopkins University Press. Retrieved from https://www.jstor.org/stable/23352253.

Nasir, R. (2009). Muslim Women's Perception in Delhi on the Religio-Cultural and Non-Cultural Indicators Associated with Status. *Man in India*, 89(1-2), 142-149.

National Family Health Survey (NFHS-4). (2017). Ministry of Health & Family Welfare. *International Institute for Population Sciences*. Retrieved from https://dhsprogram.com/pubs/pdf/FR339/FR339.pdf.

Niu, X., & Laidler, K. A. J. (2015). Understanding domestic violence against Muslim women in China. *Feminist criminology*, 10(1), 92-112. doi: org/10.1177/1557085114536766.

North East Network. (2015). Domestic Violence in Rural Assam. Retrieved from https://northeastnetwork.org/wp-content/uploads/2021/10/1154-NEN-DV-Report.-UNHEARD.pdf.

North East Today. (2021). NCRB Stats Point towards High Crime Rates against Women in Cachar. Retrieved from https://www.northeasttoday.in/2021/11/11/assam-ncrb-stats-point-towards-high-crime-rates-against-women-in-cachar/.

Nowrin, N. (2021). Prevalence and Key Risk Factors of Spousal Violence in the Canadian Muslim Community. *Journal of Integrated Sciences*, 1(3), 1-24.

Ondicho, T. G. (2000). Battered Women: A Socio-Legal Perspective of their Experiences in Nairobi.*African Study Monographs,* 21(1), 35-44. Retrieved from http://hdl.handle.net/11295/39046.

Oyewuwo-Gassikia O, B. (2016). American Muslim Women and Domestic Violence Service Seeking: A Literature Review.*Affilia*, 31(4), 450-462. doi:10.1177/0886109916654731.

Parida, P. K. (2009). Women's Health and Domestic Violence. *Published by A.S Saini for Dominant Publishers and distributors. Printed at orient offset, Delhi*, ISBN 81-7888-683-9.

Pathak, B. (2009). Domestic Violence: Need for Social Awareness. Published by A.S Saini for Dominant Publishers and distributors. *Printed at orient off set, Delhi,* ISBN 81-7888-683-9.

Pathak, V. (2020). Note on Gender Discrimination and Human Rights Abuses in the Khap Area. In Bhange. C.B., M., Jangir, M. & Ansari, N. A. (Eds.). Various Dimensions of Women Empowerment in India. *Bharati Publications New Delhi-110002 (India)*, 72-76.

Pearson, I., Butler, N., Yelgezekova, Z., Nihlén, Å., Yordi-Aguirre, I., Quigg, Z., & Stöckl, H.(2021). Emerging responses implemented to prevent and respond to violence against women and children in WHO European member states during the COVID-19 pandemic: a scoping review of online media reports. *BMJ Open*, 11(4), e045872. doi:10.1136/bmjopen-2020-045872.

Perez, A. (2018). Social Work Students' Perceptions of Intimate Partner Violence Victims Who Stay With Their Abusers. *Electronic Theses, Projects, and Dissertations*, 665. Retrieved from https://scholarworks.lib.csusb.edu/etd/665.

Personal Law (Shariat) Application Act. (1937). Retrieved from https://legislative.gov.in/sites/default/files/A1937-26.pdf.

Peterman, A. & O'Donnell, M. (2021). Violence against Women and Children during COVID-19. *Centre for Global Development*. Retrieved from https://www.cgdev.org/publication/covid-19-and-violene-against-women-and-children-second-research-round.

Policy Brief. (2020).The Impact of COVID-19 on Women. Population Foundation of India. Retrieved from https://populationfoundation.in/wp-content/uploads/2020/07/Policy-Brief_Impact-of-COVID-19-on-Women.pdf.

Pre-Conception & Pre-Natal Diagnostic Techniques Act. (1994). Retrieved from https://www.indiacode.nic.in/bitstream/123456789/8399/1/pre-conception-pre-natal-diagnostic-techniques-act-1994.pdf.

Prescila, S. S. (2014). Domestic Violence against Women in India: A Family Menace. *Indian Journal of Applied Research,* 4(12), ISSN 2249-555X.

Priscilla, O. (2005). Women in Islamic societies, a selected review of social scientific literature. *Washington, D.C.: Federal Research Division, Library of Congress*, Retrieved from https://www.loc.gov/rr/frd/pdf-files/Women_Islamic_Societies.pdf.

Priyanka, R., & Jyoti, S. (2014).Practice of Dowry and Domestic Violence. *Research Journal of Recent Sciences,* 3, 95-98, ISSN 2277-2502.

Rajkumari, B., & Keisham. (2016). Violence against Women: An Emerging Health Issue in North East India. *Annals of International Medical and Dental Research*, 2(6).

Rampal, S. (2014). Deprivation of Women's Human Rights and Strategies for Resolution. *Zenab Banu, Kanishka Publishers, New Delhi*, 240.

Rastogi, M., & Therly, P. (2006). Dowry and its link to Violence against Women in India. *Trauma, Violence, & Abuse,* 7(1), 66-77. doi:10.1177/1524838005283927.

Raymond, W. (1900). Mohammedan Law in India: Its Origin and Growth, *Journal of the Society of Comparative Legislation*, 2(1), 27-44.

Razack, S. H. (2004). Imperilled Muslim women, dangerous Muslim men and civilised Europeans: Legal and social responses to forced marriages. *Feminist legal studies*, 12(2), 129-174.

Retrieved from http://rchiips.org/nfhs/NFHS-3%20Data/VOL 1/India_volume_I_corrected_17oct08.pdf.

Riley, K. M. (2011). Violence in the Lives of Muslim Girls and Women in Canada. Creating a Safe Space for Dialogue, Reflection, and Research Symposium, 22-24.

Rukmini, S. (2010). Women's Subjectivities of Suffering and Legal Rhetoric on Domestic Violence: Fissures in the Two Discourses. *Indian Journal of Gender Studies*, 17(3) 375–401. doi:10.1177/097152151001700304.

Saghir, H.A., Tabassum., Amir, M., Arshad, A.S., Cheema., & Cheema, S. (2011). Gender and Violence: A Rising Issue. *The Journal of Animal & Plant Sciences*, 21(3), 632-634, ISSN 1018-7081.

Sakhi, One Stop Centre, Under Department of Social Welfare run by District Administration of Cachar, Panchayat Road, Silchar, Cachar, Assam-788005. Retrieved from https://www.facebook.com/pages/category/Government-Organization/ One-Stop-Centre-Sakhi-Cachar-670451279965257/.

Salarifar, M. R. (2009). An Explanation of the Causes and Grounds of Domestic Violence. *Studies in Islam and Psychology*, 3(4), 7-41.

Salter, M. (2013). Multi-Perpetrator Domestic Violence. *Trauma, Violence, & Abuse,* 15(2), 102–112. doi:10.1177/1524838013511542.

Sarma, B. B. (2014). Domestic Violence against Women in India: A Painful Experience of Human Rights Scandal, Samanvaya, *An Annual Research Journal Of Business Studies*, 4, ISSN 2249-4545.

Saumya, V. (2019). Muslim Women in India: A Struggle for Dignified Existence. *Amity International Journal of Juridical Sciences,* 5, 75-87.

Schuler, S.R., Bates, L.M., & Islam, F. (2008). Women's Rights, Domestic Violence, and Recourse Seeking in Rural Bangladesh. *Sage Publication*, 326-345.Retrieved fromhttp://vaw.sagepub.com hosted at http://online.sagepub.com. doi: 10.1177/1077801207313970.

Sepali, G., Brenda, R., & Cristina, C.(2012). Violence against Women: An Exploration of the Physical and Mental Health Trends among Immigrant and Refugee Women in Canada. *Hindawi Publishing Corporation Nursing Research and Practice,*20(12), 15. doi:10.1155/2012/434592.

Shahzadi, N. K., Qureshi, M. B. H., & Islam, M. (2012). Effect of Domestic Violence on Women Psychology in Pakistan. *Language in India*, 12, 1-19, ISSN 1930-2940.

Shakeel, A., & Malika, M. (2010). Modern Education and Socio-Economic Change: A case study of Muslim Women in Pune city, India. *Journal of Gender Studies,* 16 (1), 47-75. doi:10.1177/097152150801600103.

Shalu, N. (2020). COVID-19: India's Response to Domestic Violence Needs Rethinking. Retrieved from https://ssrn.com/abstract=3598999.

Sharma, P., & Khokhar, A. (2021). Domestic violence and coping strategies among married adults during lockdown due to coronavirus disease (COVID-19) pandemic in India: A cross-sectional study. *Disaster Med Public Health Prep*. doi: org/10.1017 dmp.2021.59.

Sharmin, S.S., & Azad, M.M. (2018).Laws of Muslim Marriage from the concept of the Holy Qur'an. *International Journal of Engineering and Applied Sciences (IJEAS).* 5(7), ISSN 2394-3661. Retrieved from https://www.ijeas.org/download_data/IJEAS0507008.pdf.

Shelter. (2021). Cycle of Violence. Retrieved from https://www.shelterforhelpinemergency.org/get-help/cycle-violence.

Siddiqui, H. Y. (1987). Muslim women in Transtion: A Social Profile. *New Delhi, Harnam publications.*

Simister, J., & Makowiec, J. (2008). Domestic Violence in India: Effects of Education. *Indian Journal of Gender Studies,* 15(3), 507–518. doi:org/10.1177/097152150801500304.

Special Marriage Act. (1954). Parliament of India. Retrieved from https://legislative.gov.in/sites/default/files/A1954-43_1.pdf.

Statement of Crime against women for the year 2005 to December 2020: Government of Assam, Home & Political, Assam Police. Retrieved from https://police.assam.gov.in/information-services/crime-data.

Statistical Handbook of Assam. (2014). Directorate of Economics and Statistics, Govt. of Assam. Retrieved from https://des.assam.gov.in/sites/default/files/menu/document/ecostat_medhassu_in/Statistical%20Hand%20Book%20Assam%2C%202014.pdf.

Sturmey, P. (Eds.). (2017). The Wiley handbook of violence and aggression. *John Wiley & Sons Limited,* ISBN 9781119057574. doi:10.1002/9781119057574.

Swadhar Greh (A Scheme for Women in Difficult Circumstances) Home, Wodwichee, Silchar, Cachar, Assam. Retrived from https://wcd.nic.in/schemes/swadhar-greh-scheme-women-difficult-circumstances.

Tahir, M. (2000). Crime against women- A regional analysis. In Mehertaj Begum (Eds.), *Human rights in India: Issues and perspective*. New Delhi: APH Publishing House.

Tahir, M. D. (2017). Domestic Violence against Women in Pakistan and its Solution from an Islamic Perspective: A Critical and Analytical Study.

Taub,A. (2020). A New Covid-19 Crisis: Domestic Abuse Rises Worldwide. *The New York Times*. Retrieved from https://www.nytimes.com/2020/04/06/world/coronavirus-domestic-violence.html.

Tenkorang, E. Y., Owusu. A. Y., Yeboah, E. H., & Bannerman, R. (2013). Factors Influencing Domestic and Marital Violence against Women in Ghana. *J Fam,* 28, 771–781.

Terra, P.(2017). The Impact of Witnessing Domestic Violence on Children: A Systematic Review. Retrieved from Sophia, the St. Catherine University repository website. Retrieved from https://sophia.stkate.edu/msw_papers/776.

The Child Marriage Restraint Act. (1929). Retrieved from http://chdslsa.gov.in/right_menu/act/pdf/childmarriage.pdf.

The Commission of Sati (Prevention) Act. (1987). Retrieved from https://www.indiacode.nic.in/bitstream/123456789/1814/2/A1988-03.pdf.

The Dowry Prohibition Act. (1961). Retrieved from https://www.indiacode.nic.in/bitstream/123456789/5556/1/dowry_prohibition.pdf.

The Factories Act. (1948). Retrieved from https://labour.gov.in/sites/default/files/Factories_Act_1948.pdf.

The Hindu Marriage Act. (1955). Retrieved from https://highcourtchd.gov.in/hclscc/subpages/pdf_files/4.pdf.

The Hindu Succession Act. (1956). Retrieved from http://ncwapps.nic.in/acts/TheHinduSuccessionAct1956.pdf.

The Immoral Traffic (Prevention) Act. (1956). Retrieved from https://www.indiacode.nic.in/bitstream/123456789/6818/1/ind93633.pdf.

The Indecent Representation of Women (Prohibition) Act. (1986). Retrieved from https://legislative.gov.in/sites/default/files/A1986-60_0.pdf.

The Medical Termination of Pregnancy Act. (1971). Retrieved from https://tcw.nic.in/Acts/MTP-Act-1971.pdf.

The National Commission for Women Act. (1990). Retrieved from https://wcd.nic.in/sites/default/files/ncwact.pdf.

The Prohibition of Child Marriage Act. (2006). Retrieved from https://legislative.gov.in/sites/default/files/A2007-06.pdf.

The Protection of Women from Domestic Violence Act. (2005). Retrieved from https://www.indiacode.nic.in/bitstream/123456789/15436/1/protection_of_women_from_domestic_violence_act%2C_2005.pdf.

The Special Marriage Act. (1954). Retrieved from https://legislative.gov.in/sites/default/files/A1954-43_1.pdf.

The Times of India. (2016). Violence against women on the rise in state. Retrieved from https://timesofindia.indiatimes.com/city/guwahati/violence-against-women-on-the-rise-in-state/articleshow/53276127.cms.

Tod, D., & Lavallee, D. (2011).Social psychological theories and models. McLachlan, S., Chan, D.K.C., Keatley, D., & Hagger, M. (Eds.),The Psychology of Strength and Conditioning, *Routledge,* 26, ISBN 9780203855188.

Uddin, M. M. (1985). Divorce under Islamic Law. *Cochin University Law Review*, 315-349.

United Nations General Assembly. (1957). Convention on the Nationality of Married Women. *United Nations Human Rights. Office of the High Commissioner.*Retrieved from https://treaties.un.org/doc/treaties/1958/08/19580811%2001-34%20am/ch_xvi_2p.pdf.

United Nations General Assembly. (1967). Declaration on the Elimination of Discrimination against Women. *United Nations Human Rights. Office of the High Commissioner. Retrieved from* https://www.eods.eu/library/UNGA_Declaration%20Women_1967_en.pdf.

United Nations General Assembly. (1979). Convention on the Elimination of all Forms of Discrimination against Women. Retrieved from https://www.ohchr.org/documents/professionalinterest/cedaw.pdf.

United Nations. (1948). Universal Declaration of Human Rights. Retrieved from https://www.jus.uio.no/lm/en/pdf/un.universal.declaration.of.human.rights.1948.portrait.letter.pdf.

Wagman, J.A., Donta, B., Ritter, J., Naik, D. D., Nair, S., Saggurti, N., & Raj, A. & Silverman, J.G. (2016). Husband's Alcohol Use, Intimate Partner Violence, and Family Maltreatment of Low-Income Postpartum Women in Mumbai, India. *Journal of Interpersonal Violence,* 1(27), 1. doi:10.1177/0886260515624235.

Waheed, A. (2009).Dowry among Indian Muslims: Ideals and Practices. *Indian Journal of Gender Studies*, 16(1), 47–75. doi:10.1177/097152150801600103.

Wang, L. (2016). Factors influencing attitude toward intimate partner violence. Aggression and Violent Behavior, 29, 72–78. doi: org/10.1016/j.avb.2016.06.005.

WHO, 2013, London School of Hygiene & Tropical Medicine South African Medical Research Council. Prevalence and health effects of intimate partner violence and non-partner sexual violence Global and regional estimate of violence against women. ISBN 978 924 1564625.Retrieved fromhttps://www.who.int/publications/i/item/9789241564625.

World Health Organization Report on Human Reproduction Programme on COVID-19 and violence against women what the health sector/system can do. Retrieved from https://apps.who.int/iris/bitstream/handle/10665/331699/WHO-SRH-20.04-eng.pdf?ua=1.

World Health Organization. (2007). *WHO Multicountry Study on Women's Health and Domestic Violence against Women*. Geneva, Switzerland.

Yucel, S. (2019). Muslim Women, Domestic Violence, and Psychotherapy. *Australian Journal of Islamic Studies*, 4(1), 72-74, ISSN 2207-4414.

Zubaidi, N. (2015). Socio cultural Theory. PhD Conference: Researching Language, University of Melbourne. doi:10.13140/RG.2.1.2642.1921.

Appendix

Annexure A-I Interview Schedule for the Muslim Women Victims of Domestic Violence

Section A: Demographic and Socio-Economic Profile

1. Age of the Respondent

a) 18-22 b) 23-27 c) 28-32 d) 33-37 e) 38-42 f) Above42

2. Age of Marriage

a) 16-20 b) 21-25 c) 26-30 d) Above30

3. Nature of marriage

a) Arranged marriage b) Love marriage with the consent of family c) love marriage without the consent of family

4. No. of times the respondent married?

a) First b) Second c) Multiple

5. The reported violence is from which marriage?

a) First b) Second c) Multiple

6. Marital Status of the Respondent

a) Married b) Divorced c) Separated d) Widow

7. Caste

a) MOBC b) General

8. Type of Family

a) Nuclear b)Joint

9. Do you have children?

a) Yes b) No

10. If yes, how many children do you have?

a) One b) Two c) More than two

11. Educational standardof the Respondents

a) Illiterate b) Primary c) MiddleSchool d) HSLC e) Graduate f) Post Graduate

12. Occupational background of the Respondents

a) Homemaker b) Job in Govt &Pvt. Sector c) Labourer d) housemaid e) Businesswomen

13. MonthlyIncome of the family

a) Less than Rs. 5000(c)Rs. 5001- Rs.8000(d) Rs.8001-Rs.11000(e)Above Rs. 11000

14. Personal Monthly Income

a) No income b) Less than Rs. 3000 c) Rs.3001-Rs.6000 d) Above6000

Section B:Nature and Extent of Domestic Violence

15. What is your perception about the nature of domestic violence?

a) Repeated quarrel on less important issues
b) Superiority feeling on sexual matter
c) Suspecting character
d) Physical abuse on trivial issues
e) Insulting in front of others
f) Constant mental harassment
g) Scolding without valid reason

16. According to you who are the instigators of Domestic Violence?

a) Mother-in-law b) Father-in-law c) Brother-in-law d) Sister-in-law e) Relativesof Husband f) Any other

17. Rate of recurrence of Domestic Violence

a) On daily basis b) Once or more episodesinaweek c) once or more episodes in a month d) Occasionally

18. How long you have been facing domestic violence?

a) <1year b) 1-2years c) 2-3years d) 3-4years e) 4-5years f) >5years

Section C: Factors leading to Domestic Violence

19. Health Factor

a) Suspicion of psychological disorder by abusers
b) Unable to procure children
c) Adverse health issues
d) Stress and Anxiety of husband
e) Physical deformity of husband
f) Adverse health issues of husband
g) Other

20. Economic Factor

a) Meagre family income
b) Unemployed husband
c) Non acceptance of wife's economic independence
d) Control over wife's full income
e) Repeatedlyforcingthewifeforbringingmoneyandothermaterialsfromherparents.

21. Sexual Factor

a) Physical limitations to respond to the sexual needs of husband
b) Mismatch in desire to have the amount of sex
c) Male superiority over female on sexual matters
d) Forced sexual intercourse

22. Emotional Factor

a) Criticism for alleged low intelligence status
b) Humiliating for no convincing reasons
c) Scolding for expressing views on family or financial matters
d) Repeated nagging on small and negligible matters
e) Suspects extramarital relations
f) Restrictions in maintaining relationship with parents
g) Compelling to feel guilty for no obvious fault
h) Holding wife responsible for the ill health of kids
i) Holding wife responsible for kids poor academic performance
j) Restrictionofopeninteractionwithherchildrenbyin-lawsHusband'salcohol dependence

23. Religious Factor

a) Misinterpretation of teachings of Quran
b) Blindly following teachings of religious leaders
c) Misguided about the supremacy of men over women
d) Non adherence to traditional dresses
e) Restriction in adopting modern way of life.

Section D:Factors inducing Violence

24. What are the types of violence faced by the respondent

a) Physical b) Emotional c) Mental

25. Modes of physical violence

a) Shoving roughly
b) Hurling objects towards the victim
c) Twisting armor slapping
d) Kicking or dragging
e) Using a weapon to cause injury
f) Attempting murder

26. Modes Emotional Violence

a) Threatening to divorce
b) Showing in different attitude towards the health of the victim
c) Threatening to commit suicide by the husband
d) Threat to use physical force
e) Threatening to remarry
f) Threatening to cast out of home
g) Threatening to harm children physically
h) Social defamation of the victim's parents

27. What is your immediate reaction to domestic violence?

a) Causing self mutilation
b) Screaming and crying
c) Breaking objects
d) Urge to leave the house
e) Feeling of helplessness
f) Urge to commit suicide
g) Any other (please specify)

Annexure A-II Interview Schedule for the Muslim Women Victims of Domestic Violence

Section A: Effects of casual factors

1. Do you think mentioned casual factors had any effects?

a) Yes b) No

2. If yes, how did this causal factor affect you?

a) Affected family relations
b) Affected Sexual relations
c) Affected Children's wellbeing
d) Affected social relations
e) Affected mental health

3. Effect on family relations

a) Marital relationship is under pressure and tension
b) Creation of a fearful environment
c) Ignoring wife's wishes in family matters
d) Communication gaps leading to constant misunderstandings
e) Loss of trust and respect between husband &wife
f) Conflict on minor issues
g) Family peace is destroyed
h) Creating misunderstanding between the in-laws

4. Effect on sexual relations

a) Diminished sexual feelings for husband
b) Decreased urge for sexual encounters
c) Sex under compulsion

d) Decline in sexual satisfaction

e) Feeling of intense repulsionon husband's sexual advances

5. Effect on children's wellbeing

a) Poor performance in study and school

b) Difficulty in sleeping properly

c) Development of adverse traits (anxiety, fear, depression)

d) Showing aggressive/ antisocial behaviour

e) Impedance in reaching developmental milestones (Speech, conversation etc)

f) Poor self esteem & self confidence

6. Effect on social relations

a) Limited communication with family

b) Ashamed of facingneighbours

c) Avoidance of social gatherings

d) Lost contact with relatives, friends

e) Facing social isolation

f) Social defamation of victim's family members

7. Effect on mental health

a) Under constant stress

b) Severe anxiety and depression

c) Frequent mood swings

d) Sleep disturbance

e) Suicidal tendency

f) Increased lethargy and fatigability

Section B:Help seeking approach of the respondent

8. Did you share about this abusive situation with anybody?

a) Yes b)No

9. If yes, whom did you inform initially?

a) Parents/ownfamily members b) Close Friends c) Close relatives d)Close neighbour groups

10. Did you seek any help from them?

a) Yes b) No

11. Did you receive any help from them?

a) Yes b) No

12. Were you given any suggestion by your in-laws?

a) Yes b) No

13. If yes, what are those?

a) Mutual agreement by both families to resolve issues
b) Ask for legal advice
c) Approach Police
d) Approaching Social-legal organisations
e) Temporary disconnection with husband and in-laws
f) Get divorce
g) Any other

14. Was there any suggestion by your parents/family members?

a) Yes b) No

15. Ifyes, what were those?

a) Mutual agreement by both families to resolve issues
b) Ask for legal advice
c) Approach Police
d) Approaching Social-legal organisations
e) Temporary disconnection with husband and in-laws
f) Get divorce

Section C:Reporting of Cases

16. What are the organisations approached for reporting of cases?

a) Police Department
b) Family Court
c) Local Panchayat
d) District Court
e) District Social Welfare department
f) Social organisations

17. What services were you seeking?

a) Family Counseling
b) Rescue
c) Shelter
d) Legal assistance

18. Were you provided with any of the above-mentioned services?

a) Yes b) No

19. Were these organisations able to intervene your problem?

a) Yes b) No c) Partially

20. Were these services satisfactory?

a) Yes b) No

If no, were you thinking about approaching other social organisation for seeking help?

a) Yes b) No

Annexure A-III Interview Schedule to Understand Victim's Perception

Section A: Awareness about Support Providing Agencies

1. Were you aware about the support providing agencies working on domestic violence issues?

a) Yes b) No

2. If yes, from whom you have come to know about these organisations

a) Parents/family members b) Government officials c) Friendsd) News paper e) Local clubs

3. Have you approached any of these organisations for registering your case and seeking support?

a) Yes b) No

4. If yes, what are those organisations?

5. Were you aware about the services provided by the organisation?

a) Yes b) No

6. Have you received any service from these organisations?

a) Yes b) No

7. What type of services you have received?

a) Emergency Response and Rescue Services
b) Medical Assistance
c) Assistance to women in lodging FIR/NCR/DIR
d) Psycho-social support/counselling
e) Legal aid and counselling

f) Shelter

g) Vocational Training

8. Are these services common to women of all religion?

a) Yes b) No

9. Are these services specifically designed to address different religions?

a) Yes b) No

10. If yes, what are the special provisions available for Muslim women

Section B: Problem faced in Receiving the Services

11.Have you faced any problem while receiving these services?

a) Yes b) No

12. Do you think that these services could solve your problem?

a) Yes, totally b) Yes, partially c) No

13. If partially, what aspects were left to be covered?

14. If no, what alternatives have you adopted?

a) Living with husband and compromising
b) Living with parents and trying to restart life
c) Living alone and working
d) Reached out to different organisation for support
e) Any other

15. What compels you to stay in abusive relationship?

a) No alternative house to stay
b) Children's future
c) Parents repute
d) Hoping for better future
e) Giving a second chance to start a fresh

Section C:Perception of the Respondents about the services provided

16. According to you which service did you find to be the most beneficial and why?

17. In-spite of the problems, are you satisfied with the services received?

a) Yes b) No

18. If yes, what are those services which satisfied you the most?

19. If no, mention those services which you were not satisfied with.

20. Please suggest measures to reduce domestic violence.

Annexure A-IV Interview Schedule for Support Providing Agencies

Section A: Profile of the Organisation

1. Name of the Organisation
2. Background of the Organisation
3. Objectives of the Organisation
4. Organisational Structure
5. Sources of Fund
6. Functions of the Organisation
7. Types of cases registered in the organisation

a) Domestic violence b) Kidnapping c) Trafficking
d) Destitute women e) Property related problems f) Women in difficult circumstances
g) Shelter less women

Section B:Service components of the organisation

8. What are the services provided to the victims by the organisation?
9. Do you follow any criteria for selection of cases?

a) Yes b) No

10. What is the process of dealing with cases?
11. Are there any religious considerations for dealing with the cases?

a) Yes b) No

12. Do you collaborate with other organisations for delivering services?

a) Yes b) No

13. Do you need to report about the services delivered?

a) Yes b) No

Section C: Problems faced by the support providing agencies

14. Do you receive fund timely to run the organisation?

a) Yes b) No c) Sometime

15. Do you get support from the stakeholders in delivering the services?

a) Yes b) No c) Sometime

16. Do you face problems in delivering services under each component?

a) Yes b) No

17. If yes, what are the problems faced under each component

18. Have you faced any confrontation on religious grounds while dealing with such cases?

a) Yes b) No c) Sometime

19. Do you feel the success and failure of your services have any religious implications?

20. How do you respond to these problems?

Section D:Suggestions & Future Plans

21. Please provide suggestions for improving service delivery under each component.

22. What are your future plans?